Tales of
Old Cumbria

Tales of
Old Cumbria

~

William Amos

With illustrations by Don Osmond

COUNTRYSIDE BOOKS

NEWBURY, BERKSHIRE

COUNTRYSIDE BOOKS
3 Catherine Road
Newbury, Berkshire

ISBN 1 85306 378 9

Designed by Mon Mohan
Cover illustration by Colin Doggett
Map by Trevor Yorke

Produced through MRM Associates Ltd., Reading
Printed by J.W. Arrowsmith Ltd., Bristol

Contents

N

Netherby

CARLISLE

Wigton

EDEN VALLEY

Croglin

Caldbeck   Calthwaite

PENRITH

Threlkeld

Ullswater

Ennerdale   Buttermere   △ Helvellyn   Shap

Easedale

Wasdale   Langdale   Grasmere
Miterdale   Rydal

Seathwaite   Tebay

Clarke

Coniston
Water   Bowness
Windermere

KENDAL

Oxenholme   Dent

Lindale

Ulverston   Cartmel

BARROW
IN
FURNESS

Piel Island

Introduction

HAD you been in Ambleside in the 1820s or '30s you might have seen a gaunt figure hurrying to the post office for by no means the first time, there to seek the return of a packet just posted as he wished to amend the contents. It would be pointed out to him that this was against regulations, but finally an exception would grudgingly be made. After all, the customer was Westmorland's distributor of government stamps. He was also William Wordsworth, ever a perfectionist, wanting to improve one of his poems.

I sometimes wonder if the poet's less appealing verse is that which he failed to retrieve in time from the post office. The concern of the ruffled postmaster, however, was his own coercion into flouting Post Office rules. He would rather have Coleridge drunk, he said, than Wordsworth sober.

Happily, no such hassle has attended the posting of these Cumbrian stories, likewise despatched from Ambleside.

In presenting these tales – a mix of old favourites, others long forgotten but worth recalling and a few not to be found elsewhere – I must acknowledge my debt to earlier chroniclers, to John West of Grasmere for alerting me to some I would otherwise have missed and to John Dawson of Coniston for research in the more recent past. This book would have been the poorer without them.

Will our own times yield a further harvest of tales worth telling? I like to think so, encouraged by incidents such as one which took place at Coniston not so long ago – in 1970, should you raise an eyebrow in disbelief.

On the outskirts of that village is a farm which had long been run by the Oliphant family, and it was to Coniston police station that a girl from London made her way one day to report some stray beasts in the road. They were half a mile outside the village, she said, indicating the direction.

'Ah, yes,' said the officer, 'they'll be Oliphant's.'

'Oh, no – they're cows.'

William Amos
Little Langdale, Autumn 1996

The
Wild Dog
of Ennerdale

IT was never known to bark or growl, it performed its operations with almost surgical precision and it had the cunning of a fox. This was the wild dog of Ennerdale which made its first appearance in the valley on or about 10th May 1810, and swiftly became the scourge of the neighbourhood.

Where it had come from, nobody knew. It was believed to be a gipsies' stray and seemed to be a cross between a mastiff and a greyhound, tawny in colour, its smooth hair streaked with markings like those of a tiger. And with its arrival no sheep in the district was safe – in a single night it would kill as many as seven or eight, feasting on the animals while they were still alive.

Scared off by a shepherd during one attack, it was found to have torn its victim's flesh from the ribs behind the shoulder, exposing the heart, which was still beating. But the dog was seldom caught in the act, usually confining its activities to darkness and never striking the same flock twice on successive nights. Instead, it would move on to fresh prey two or three miles away. Almost invariably it went first for the jugular vein, which was usually found to have been opened on the same side of the neck.

Pursued by shepherds, their collies and hounds, the wild dog would outrun the lot. 'Many an enlivening gallop has been enjoyed at the unusual season of summer', it was recorded half a century later, 'by occasional horsemen who have been crossed and surprised by the chase in full cry. So exciting did it become, that when the cheering echoes gave notice that the game was on foot, horses were hastily unyoked from carts or ploughs, and mounted bareback and ridden as long as they could go, and then left to take their chance whilst their riders continued the chase on foot.

'It was no uncommon sight to see a score or two of men running at the top of their speed after the hounds, without hats or coats, to the wonder of the inhabitants of the districts they passed through; and many well-to-do yeomen have been obliged to strangers for hospitable refreshment at the end of an unsuccessful chase, ending many miles from home, or the starting place, they having joined the hunt in their hurry with empty pockets.'

For its resting-places the dog chose spots offering a good view on all sides, usually settling on rocks where its dingy colour made it difficult to descry even when it moved to steal away. At first it was thought that persistent harrying would soon drive it out of the district. A chase covering as many as 15 miles would be assumed to have done the trick. Then a day or two later another savaged sheep would be discovered.

Pursuing hounds were treated with disdain by the

fleeing dog. Having taken their measure, it would wait for them and then give their leader such a mauling that the rest would hold back. To counter the menace, night-shifts were organised, volunteers taking turns to watch the fells, guns at the ready. Bitches on heat were tethered in an attempt to entice the wild dog within shooting range, but the fugitive kept its distance; sheep carcases were poisoned, but left untouched. Nothing seemed to work.

Harvesting was skimped, cows went unmilked, horses unfed as the constant strain of keeping watch overnight took its toll on the community. Willy Jackson of Swinside came the nearest to success when, leaving his home with his loaded gun, he saw the dog cocking its leg against a thistle. It was only 30 yards away. Willy could hardly miss. Then there was a click – his gun had misfired – and the dog was off.

When sheepshearing came round in July, a subscription was launched to finance the formation of the swiftest and most ferocious pack of hounds that could be obtained. John Russell, a Whitehaven brewer with 3,000 acres under sheep in Ennerdale, offered free ale to the night patrols and £10 for the wild dog's capture, dead or alive. And between them the sheepfarmers raised some £12 for refreshments for the wilting watchers.

A particularly determined effort was mounted one July morning when about 200 men with hounds spread out in couples to scour the Kinniside fells. The wild dog was spotted, and the view halloo from some 40 or 50 men brought the hounds to the scent. Their quarry led them to the heights above Wastwater, to Browny Edge and Stockdale Moor and thence to a cornfield at Priorscale. By that time only about 40 men and a few hounds had stayed the course. Watchers were posted

13

round the field while more hounds were collected. But instead of resting, as expected, the dog had stolen away. It was slowly traced through Calder and Seascale and then, as dusk fell, it was lost at Drigg.

Further sightings followed in the ensuing weeks, and more sheep became the dog's prey. In one chase extending to nearly 20 miles, it was pursued from the Kinniside fells through Lamplugh and Dean. Then it crossed the river Marron a few times, rested in a plantation near Clifton and was finally lost near the river Derwent.

Another intensive watch was mounted on a Saturday night by men posted on the high fells with guns and dogs. Nothing was seen of the dog, so the men came down at about 11 am on Sunday and dispersed at Swinside Lane end. A few minutes later Willy Lamb gave the view halloo; he had spotted the dog crossing a wooded ghyll, and it now fled with the hounds in full cry.

'The hunt passed Ennerdale church during service,' says a contemporary account, 'and the male part of the congregation, liking the cry of the hounds better than the sermon, ran out and followed. It has been said that the Rev. Mr. Ponsonby could not resist and went in pursuit as far as he was able.' The run ended at Fitz Mill, near Cockermouth, in a storm which continued to lash the tired pursuers and their hounds throughout their 12-mile return journey.

The following morning a farmer saw the dog steal into a hedge and lie down. Charging his gun with swan shot, he crept closer to make sure of his aim, but the dog heard him and ran, the gun-pellets inflicting no more than a light peppering.

THE WILD DOG OF ENNERDALE

More hunts and narrow escapes followed. In one chase the dog led its pursuers from the head of Ennerdale Water to St Bees, via the Kinniside fells and Egremont. A violent storm then broke, and the hunters who had left their coats and waistcoats on the fells returned home saturated. 'Some of them took colds which remained with them till death', it was recorded.

A woman visiting Birkmoss went to pick apples in an orchard near the river Ehen, but returned in a fright, saying she had seen 'an awful looking wild beast' lying in long grass beneath one of the apple trees. John Steel of Birkmoss, who had just returned from his watch on the fells, posted a man to keep an eye on the dog while he hallooed for the hounds. The pack assembled within 30 minutes, but the dog had meanwhile crept unseen to another hiding place. There it was soon found and started with the hounds at its heels, bolting between the crooked legs of the deaf and elderly Jack Wilson who was stooping to gather sticks, unaware of what was going on around him. Having inadvertently come nearer than anyone to the wild dog of Ennerdale, which had passed right under his nose, he afterwards said he thought it was a lion. That chase, too, ended without success near St Bees.

Another time, when the dog was sighted in a wood, hunters including 13 men with guns stationed themselves round the copse where their quarry was believed to be lurking. When it broke cover and ran towards Will Rothery, who was in position, gun in hand, the man was so overcome by his first view of the creature that he stepped back and allowed it to pass unharmed. All he could say was 'What a dog!'

As summer progressed and the corn ripened it was

decided to abandon the chase for two or three weeks until after the harvest. That would remove at least one of the dog's favourite hiding places, which the hunters couldn't enter lest they damage the crops.

Then, on 12th September, old John Patrickson saw the dog going into a cornfield. He quietly raised the alarm and enough men were soon mustered, along with hounds, to surround the field, but not all of them had guns. A delay was whispered round while more weapons were fetched to ensure that everyone was armed. Only Patrickson, however, was able to get a shot at it when the dog was finally disturbed and ran from hiding.

Wounded in the hindquarters, it consequently lost a little of its speed. This enabled the hounds to keep up with it, although none dared to close with their quarry. It now led the chase to the river Ehen, by a circuitous route taking in Kinniside fells, Eskat, Arlecdon, Asby, Rowrah and Stocklow Hall.

The dog was taking a dip in the river, the hounds quietly looking on, when another John Steel, of Asby this time caught up with it. It was a frustrating scene – there was the quarry, with £10 on its head, but he daren't shoot lest he injure the hounds. When the dog saw him, however, it made off into Eskat woods, with Steel and the hounds in pursuit. And there, at last, he was able to shoot it.

The carcase was then carried in triumphant procession to an inn at Ennerdale Bridge, where it was found to weigh eight stone. Its stuffed skin was subsequently displayed at Hutton's Museum in Keswick. This was the dog, said an accompanying notice, that had destroyed nearly 300 sheep during its five-month Ennerdale sojourn.

Skulduggery

THE worst decision ever made by Kraster Cook and his wife Dorothy was to accept an invitation to a Christmas party. Their host was Myles Philipson, the head of a family originating from Northumberland. The Philipsons had settled near Windermere in the 15th century and had become the district's dominant landowners. The Cooks had their own farm not far from Myles Philipson's lakeside home, Calgarth Hall. They also had some land which Philipson had long been trying to buy from them, but they wouldn't sell.

After the party, Philipson announced that a silver cup was missing. The cup was subsequently found in the Cooks' home. Neighbours had a good idea of how it had come to be there, and they attached no guilt to the Cooks, an eminently respectable couple. Philipson had planted the cup at the Cooks' farm, it was believed, for reasons which soon became apparent.

Those who might have spoken up on the farming couple's behalf thought twice about doing so – the influential, property-owning Myles Philipson was not a man to be crossed. Others, obligated to him for one reason or another, and not above being bribed, were only too willing to become his witnesses.

Kraster Cook and his wife were consequently convicted of the theft and condemned to death, a

convenient arrangement for Myles Philipson as it enabled him to seize their property ... but not before Dorothy Cook had risen to her feet in the court at Kendal and delivered a warning. The land the couple's accuser had coveted would be dearly acquired, she said. As long as Calgarth Hall stood, she and her husband would haunt it night and day, until the Philipsons were no more.

After the Cooks had been hanged, two skulls appeared at Calgarth Hall, defying all efforts to get rid of them. They were thrown into the lake, they were burned, and they were ground to dust, but they kept coming back, rematerialising in various parts of the hall. It was even said that they were socially inclined, attending conventions of ghosts at Armboth House, which was later to be covered by the waters of Thirlmere.

After a while, the Philipsons gave up trying to destroy the skulls, which had selected a niche on Calgarth Hall's staircase as their preferred resting place. There they were walled in, out of sight, never to haunt the Philipsons again, for soon there were no more Philipsons left to trouble.

This, it was said, was the story behind the two skulls at Calgarth Hall – and of their existence, there is no doubt. In the 1780s it was reported that one of them had been taken to London and had yet to find its way back again. In 1819, it was stated that only one skull now remained, and it had all but crumbled away.

What was perhaps the most reliable account appeared in an 1847 handbook to the Lakes, published in Kendal. This recorded that two human skulls deposited in a window at Calgarth Hall had always been regarded as indestructible. 'The country people attributed their presence to various causes, the most popular being that some diabolical act had been committed here, and that these were the imperishable remains of some murdered persons. On that account they were viewed with awe, and were visited by young and old from several miles around.

'This credulity, however, has now vanished, and the mouldering hand of time has done what it was once believed human efforts were unable to accomplish.'

An Offcomer Extraordinary

A S every lakelander knows, unless you were born and bred here you are an 'offcomer'. Just when this word was coined and precisely what it means is open to debate. One who comes often, or from far off? A bit of both, perhaps. You are still an offcomer when you've lived here for 30 or 40 years, for the term is applied without discrimination to all who are not natives. Once an offcomer, always an offcomer. It's a fact of Lake District life.

Wordsworth excepted, most of the big names of the region – Thomas Arnold, Hugh Walpole, John Ruskin, Arthur Ransome, Beatrix Potter, Alfred Wainwright – were offcomers. So was George Constantinesco, and with a name like that he could hardly pretend to be anything else. Not that he would have bothered. He was too busy. Few knew he was here. Fewer still knew quite who he was, but those who did recognised that his was a name to be quoted in the same breath as those mentioned above. Not that George Constantinesco would have thanked them for it. He had other things to think about.

He didn't mix much, not because he was unsociable

but because he had many demands on his time, and his relaxation was Beethoven at the keyboard of his grand piano. But he liked a joke. When Coniston celebrated the coronation of King George VI with a regatta at night, participants in motor boats and dinghies were intrigued by the sudden, silent and mysterious appearance among them of an unmanned vessel with no obvious means of motive power and dressed overall with coloured lights. Somehow it seemed to know where it was going as it moved purposefully through other craft and its lights dwindled in the distance as it disappeared in the direction of the bay near Oxen House, the late Victorian dwelling to which George Constantinesco had moved from Surrey in the late 1920s.

Powered by an electric motor, the phantom vessel had been his contribution to the occasion and it was all his own work. But what else would you expect from the inventor of a £100, 100 miles to the gallon car with automatic transmission? And that was only one of George Constantinesco's accomplishments.

Had you encountered this small, neatly-dressed gentleman with a foreign accent near his home on the shore of Coniston Water, and had you inquired about his background, you would doubtless have been surprised to learn of his role in helping Britain and her allies win the First World War.

Born in Romania in 1881, the son of a professor of mathematics, he had become an engineer and had settled in England in 1910 ... after building Romania's first reinforced concrete bridge. He had subsequently applied himself to research in sonics, developing theories which he was soon to put into practice.

With the outbreak of war, German fighter pilots had a

distinct advantage. Thanks to the Fokker mechanical synchronised firing gear their machine guns could fire between the blades of an aircraft's propeller. The device wasn't perfect. If it malfunctioned the pilot would suddenly find himself minus the propeller he had shot off, but it worked well enough to be adopted by the German air force and Britain had nothing to match it.

It was at this point that George Constantinesco, by now a Royal Naval Air Service boffin, came into his own. He invented a sonic synchronised firing device that was superior to the German system and gave British pilots a devastating edge over the enemy. From 1917 it was installed as standard equipment on all British and American fighters and remained as such until the Second World War, when guns were no longer situated in planes' noses but on their wings.

Constantinesco also perfected a silent, flashless gun. Powered by the expansion of highly compressed oil, it would hurl a 200 lb projectile 1,500 yards, and years later its inventor would toy with the idea of adapting it to throw rotten tomatoes at raucous motor boats disturbing the peace of Oxen House bay.

Meanwhile, having given Britain and her allies air supremacy, he went on to apply his knowledge of sonics in other fields, developing a form of automatic transmission for vehicles. This was first demonstrated in 1923 and in the following year it was incorporated in a locomotive displayed at the British Empire Exhibition at Wembley. Then came his revolutionary, five-horse-power, two-seater car demonstrated in Paris in 1926 and using the automatic transmission which he called a gearless torque converter. If you wonder why this 100 mpg car priced at £100 wasn't a commercial success, the answer is that it had a drawback. Its top speed was 40 mph, which George Constantinesco considered fast enough for anyone.

On moving to his home near Coniston he first applied his practical bent to harnessing a beck near his house to supply electricity by means of a water turbine constructed with reinforced concrete and a biscuit tin. The device provided free electricity for 20 years, and the reason why neighbours saw little of its inventor lay in the laboratory which he built nearby. There he continued his researches – under government backing during the Second World War – and, despite failing health, right up to his death in 1965. Experimental stoves and a new form of reinforced concrete were added to his inventions, all tested in theory mathematically before they were realised in practice.

Although, in retrospect, this offcomer from further away than most can be seen to have peaked in 1916 when his synchronised firing gear had its first successful demonstration, at least his breakthrough achieved a form of permanence. The device is still to be seen at the Imperial War Museum in London, the RAF Museum in Hendon and the National Air and Space Museum in Washington.

And his stoves are still to be found around Coniston.

Bigamy in Buttermere

CAPTAIN J. BUDWORTH of London was more than impressed by the girl at the Fish Inn, Buttermere. He was bowled over. The year was 1792, and the captain was on a walking tour. He first saw Mary Robinson, the landlord's daughter, when he stepped into the pub's kitchen, where Mary was spinning yarn with her mother. At the sight of the stranger, he later recorded, she 'flew away as swift as a mountain sheep', and it was not until he returned from a ramble to Scale Force that he saw her again, when she served his dinner.

She appeared to be about 15, and never before had he seen such natural grace and beauty. 'Her hair', he noted, 'was thick and long, of a dark brown, and, though unadorned with ringlets, did not seem to want them; her face was a fine oval, with full eyes and lips as red as vermilion...'

She had never been out of the village, and he hoped she would remain there, untroubled by any ambition to leave. She looked like an angel, and he felt that the world should know about her. 'Ye travellers of the Lakes,' he wrote, 'if you visit this obscure spot, in such you will find the fair Sally of Buttermere.'

Perhaps he changed her name to avoid embarrassing her, or to spare her identification. Or maybe he didn't know she was called Mary. Whatever the case, the damage was done. His *Fortnight's Ramble to the Lakes* extolled her charms, went into three editions, and it wasn't long before Mary Robinson had visitors, Wordsworth, de Quincey and Southey among them.

This was not at all what the naive captain had intended. He had only wanted to pay tribute to the girl's beauty, leaving it to blush unseen. Now, he feared, she might be spoiled, her head turned by all this attention. And he was to blame.

So in 1798 Captain Budworth returned to Buttermere, to do what he could to redress the situation. To this end, he wrote an article which appeared in *The Gentleman's Magazine*. The girl 'has really a heavenly countenance,' he now reported, 'yet she is far from a perfect beauty, and in a few years she may even grow too large ever to have been thought what she now is...'

He revealed himself to her as the author of *A Fortnight's Ramble*, and after she had curtsied respectfully he delivered his homily. 'I rejoice in having had such an opportunity of minutely observing the propriety of your behaviour,' he told her. 'You may remember I advised you, in that book, never to leave your native valley. Your age and situation require the utmost care. Strangers will come, and have come, purposely to see you, and some of them with very bad intentions. I hope you will never suffer from them, but never cease to be on your guard. You are really not so handsome as you promised to be, and I have long wished – by conversation like this – to do away what mischief the flattering character I gave of you may expose you to. Be merry and wise.'

'I hope, Sir, I ever have,' said Mary, 'and trust I shall always take care of myself.'

Upon which the captain departed. He had done his best. Indeed, he congratulated himself, he could hardly have done more. He was not to know what was soon to transpire from the compliments his book had paid Mary Robinson.

In 1802, an apparently prosperous tourist arrived in Keswick: Colonel the Honourable Alexander Augustus Hope, MP for Linlithgow and brother of Lord Hopetoun. He subsequently went to Buttermere, seduced Mary and went through a form of marriage with her at Lorton a few months later. As she was now quite a Cumberland celebrity, newspapers reported her wedding ... to the surprise of readers in Scotland who happened to know that the real Colonel Hope was at that time in Vienna. Mary's 'husband' was an imposter.

His name was John Hatfield, and he was wanted not only for bigamy but also for forgery – he had been signing letters in the guise of an MP, thus obtaining free postage.

He came from Mottram, in Cheshire, and he had been a linen draper's traveller. He had first married an illegitimate daughter of Lord Robert Manners, on learning that she had expectations from her father. This netted him £1,500, which he frittered away upon high-living in London. Then, deserting his wife and three children, he was imprisoned in the capital for failing to pay a debt.

He now saw to it that his predicament was made known to Manners's relative, the Duke of Rutland, who settled the debt and gave him £40 besides. When the duke became Lord Lieutenant of Ireland, Hatfield went to Dublin where he passed himself off as a relation of the viceroy, running up a considerable hotel bill on the strength of this story. Exposure followed, Hatfield was imprisoned, and to avoid further trouble the duke secured his release on the condition that he left Ireland.

Hatfield next surfaced in Scarborough, representing himself as a prospective MP. Once again he incurred a large hotel bill. When the fraud was discovered through his inability to pay, he fled to London where he was caught and imprisoned again – this time for several years, until he obtained his release by persuading a gullible woman from Devon to settle his debts and marry him. In due course he abandoned her and their two children, returning from Devon to London where he began to contest Queenborough in a general election, until he was declared bankrupt and decamped again, eventually making his way to Keswick.

Now, following the exposure of his bigamous marriage, he was arrested. Pending his trial, however, he was allowed to continue fishing on Derwentwater, and from there he escaped, making his way over Sty Head Pass to Ravenglass, and thence by way of Ulverston and Chester to South Wales, where the law finally caught up with him. Meanwhile, it had emerged that during his courtship of Mary Robinson, he had also arranged to marry a young woman of independent means then living in Keswick.

Brought back to Carlisle, he was tried not for bigamy, but for forgery, and hanged in 1803.

Mary had refused to testify against him, other than to confirm that 'the man whom I had the misfortune to

The
Crier of Claife

HOW do you bury something as intangible as a spirit? I wouldn't know how to begin, but the task didn't daunt a priest called in from his chantry on the Windermere islet of Lady Holme. His assignment seemed simple enough to the residents seeking his help. Priests exorcised ghosts, so he was the man for the job. He must rid them of the Claife Crier.

Claife Heights look down on Lake Windermere from the west, and it was here that the phantom Claife Crier arose to terrorise boatmen and disrupt ferry services across Windermere from the Nab, on the east bank.

The trouble began, as trouble is apt to, on a dark and stormy night. At the Nab, a ferryman was summoned by plaintive cries of 'Boat! Boat!' from across the water. Reluctantly, he set out. He was a long time gone, and by the time he returned more prospective passengers had arrived. They were surprised to see that he was alone.

Where was his fare? What had happened? The ferryman could not say. But whatever had transpired had clearly terrified him. He had been struck dumb, and he died shortly afterwards.

More cries of 'Boat! Boat!' were heard coming from

the Claife side of the lake on subsequent nights, and now no boatman would respond. It was said that the Claife Crier was a phantom monk – the district had monks aplenty, based at outposts of Furness Abbey.

Eventually, as the unnerving cries persisted and boatmen continued to turn a deaf ear to them – probably losing genuine custom in the process – the Lady Holme priest was summoned. He duly buried the spirit in a Claife quarry, known as Claife Crier Quarry to this day, and it was said that the ghost had been laid 'for as long as ivy should be green'.

Although some suspected that the Claife Crier was responsible for the loss of a ferry and the drowning of 47 passengers and 11 horses in 1635, others pointed out that the phantom had been exorcised. But had it? People were still complaining of those disturbing cries from Claife in the 1830s, and although one account has it that the crier was exorcised in the early 19th century, this seems doubtful. The spirit's interment – botched job though it may have been – must surely have taken place prior to the 15th century, by which time there was no longer a priest on Lady Holme at the chantry which had been established in 1256.

There are those who say that the Claife Crier remains active to this day, but not at the present terminus for the ferry from the Nab. The Crier can still be heard, they say, in the vicinity of a long-redundant Windermere ferry route, from Belle Grange – formerly a Furness Abbey granary, below Claife Heights – to Low Miller-ground.

A
Cumbrian Manhunt

FOR railway buffs, Oxenholme station, on the London–Glasgow line, is of interest as one of the smallest to have a subway. For locals and visitors, it's where you change trains, taking the branch line to Kendal and Windermere. But for James Baker, Oxenholme was less than welcoming. He didn't step down from his train to the platform. He dropped off and hid in a hedge. But then it's not every passenger who arrives by goods train and is wanted for murder.

An expert housebreaker from London, Baker had teamed up with three accomplices: James Martin, a trigger-happy burglar who had already killed a police inspector in Essex; a second man whose identity was never to become known; and Anthony Benjamin Rudge, a jailbird fond of quoting the classics and proud of his part in a notorious jewellery robbery in Hatton Garden.

London had become too hot for them, so the gang had decided to plunder elsewhere. The evening of 27th October 1885 found them looting Netherby Hall, north of Carlisle. Earlier, the four had left luggage at Carlisle station to await collection – bags containing revolver ammunition, skeleton keys and a jemmy.

But at Netherby Hall things didn't go quite as the burglars had planned. Disturbed before they could snatch more than £250 worth of jewellery, they were confronted soon afterwards by a police sergeant and constable. Martin had a way with policemen. He shot them. This time he left the two officers lying on the ground, seriously but not mortally wounded.

Heading for Carlisle, the gang found the city had been cordoned off by police, blocking their escape route to the station. The fourth man now left his companions as they skirted Carlisle and walked down the railway track south of the city, hoping to clamber onto a slow-moving freight wagon.

Then a police constable appeared, took one look and challenged them. Knocking him down, they kicked him senseless and Martin and Rudge laid him across the line so that the next train would decapitate him. He owed his life to Baker, who ran back, dragged him off the track and rolled him down the embankment.

The three then hid in woods to await darkness and a chance to scramble onto a goods train unobserved. With nightfall they continued their trudge south along the railway line. At Calthwaite they decided to risk calling at the station, where Rudge inquired about trains for London and was told there would be none until 7.32 the next morning. As the three hurried off, the suspicious stationmaster sent a message to Police Constable Joseph Byrnes in nearby Plumpton.

Aware of the manhunt, Byrnes left his wife and four children and set off to seek the wanted men, who after a day without food were now enjoying bread and cheese and a drink at Plumpton's Pack Horse Inn. It was shortly after they came out of the pub that they found the village constable blocking their path. Martin promptly shot him in the head and the three bundled him over a wall.

An hour and a half later, somebody leaving the Pack Horse heard groans, found the constable behind the wall and carried him to the inn where he died shortly afterwards.

Meanwhile the trio were bypassing Penrith and continuing south. As a goods train moved slowly out of Penrith, bound for Shap and Tebay, they scrambled onto a wagon. But the guard spotted them, and as the train steamed into Tebay he jumped down and ran to alert other railwaymen. Then, backed up by engine-drivers, wagon-greasers and yardsmen, the guard moved to flush out the fugitives. They broke cover when he stumbled over one of them.

Martin was felled from behind by a length of wood wielded by the station foreman. 'What d'you mean?' he cried, getting to his feet. 'I'm looking for the robbers!'

The foreman flattened him again, and the gunman was secured by other railwaymen.

Rudge, making his escape under a railway bridge, was brought down by a well-aimed crowbar. But Baker eluded his pursuers, hiding and then boarding a goods train leaving Tebay for Lancaster.

'About two hundred and fifty yards out of Tebay, I saw someone get up on the train as it was moving,' the driver said later. 'On arriving at Oxenholme, I had the train examined to find the man, but he could not be found in any part of the train.

'We remained at Oxenholme between thirty-five and forty minutes. After leaving Oxenholme, I saw a man come out of a hedge and jump into a wagon. On arriving at Carnforth, I dropped off to see which wagon the man was in. I saw him in a wagon, looking from underneath a sheet, with his head and shoulders out ... I informed the brakeman of what I had seen, and we returned to look into the wagon. But when we got there the fellow had disappeared. We remained at Carnforth for twenty-five minutes.

'On leaving, I stood up on the tender step to see if the man tried to board the train again. I saw him come from the tank house and get into another wagon. We continued to Lancaster, where I dropped off again to see if the man was still on the train. As the train passed me slowly, I saw the man looking from under a sheet in one of the wagons. When it stopped, the man jumped out and ran.'

It was now 2.30 am, and Baker had tired of goods wagons. At Lancaster station he asked a guard, 'Is this the train for Crewe way?'

'Crewe way?' said the guard. 'Where do you want to go to?'

'Liverpool or anywhere,' Baker replied.

'Have you got a ticket? It's funny at this time of night.'

Baker explained that he had been 'sweethearting'. But he hardly seemed dressed for courting.

'I could see he had spots on his face', the guard said later, 'such as arise from blacks from an engine. Placing my hand on his shoulder I said: "You are the man that's wanted." He replied, "For what?" and tried to make away. He wore an overcoat and an undercoat. He wrenched round to the right and slipped both coats, but he only got them off to the wrists.

'I seized him by each shoulder from behind and called for help. And there was plenty of help on hand, so Baker was soon under arrest.'

The trial of Martin, Rudge and Baker for murder, attempted murder and robbery followed at Carlisle, where Rudge entertained the court with his questioning of witnesses.

When one claimed he had seen the three leaving the scene of Constable Byrne's murder at 8.23 pm, Rudge asked him how he could be so sure of the time.

That was what his watch showed, said the witness, and he checked it with his clock.

'What do you set your clock by?' asked Rudge.

'I set my clock by the day.'

'I suppose all you have to do is to look at the day and then put your clock right by it? Suppose your clock stops?'

'I always have my watch at the right time.'

'Well, you are a champion! Do you set your clock by your watch?'

'Yes.'

'Then what do you set your watch by?'

'It never requires setting.'

'I wish I had it!' said Rudge.

But although he succeeded in casting doubt on the evidence of several witnesses, the prosecution had shown that the stolen jewellery had been found along the trio's escape route and the bullet which killed Byrnes had been fired by a gun of the same calibre as Martin's revolver.

As the trio were about to be sentenced to death, Rudge confessed, claimed his companions were innocent, and concluded by paying tribute to prison conditions in Carlisle which he said compared favourably with those in many jails he had known.

All three were subsequently hanged. On the scaffold at Carlisle they shook hands with each other, saying 'Goodbye, old pal,' and giving the hangman every assistance in the final pinioning and adjustment of the nooses.

James Berry, their executioner, later recorded that Baker had spent his last night writing to his sweetheart Nellie, having been troubled about her welfare:

'Just before the drop Baker cried, "Keep straight, Nellie!" and then the three men died together without a word of fear or even a quiver or a pallid cheek amongst them. The strong affection of which Baker was capable, as shown by the way in which Nellie was always uppermost in his thoughts, affected me very much. His execution was one of the saddest of my many experiences.'

Seeing Things

D O you believe in fairies? Jack Wilson of Martindale did. So did the clergy of Lamplugh, the folk of Little Langdale, Ravenglass, Stainton, Lanercost, Penrith and many another Cumbrian settlement. For them fairies were simply a fact of life.

Jack Wilson believed in them because he saw them and witnessed their departure, never to return. His account, recorded in 1857, tells how on a moonlit night, while crossing Sandwick Rigg, he came upon a large group of fairies dancing.

At first they didn't see him, so he crept closer to observe them. From their midst a ladder rose from the ground, disappearing into a cloud. Then the fairies spotted him and scurried up to the cloud, drawing their ladder up after them. 'Yance gane, ae gane, an' nivver saw mair o' them,' he said.

The presence of little creatures was also taken for granted in Lamplugh, where a page from what was apparently a register of deaths, 1st January 1658 to 1st January 1663, records: 'Frightened to death by fairies – three.' And at The Busk in Little Langdale, obliging fairies were said to churn the butter while the family slept.

Fairy Bead Beck, near Stainton, was so called because of its oddly-shaped pebbles, some of them resembling

cups and saucers fit for fairies; and in Ravenglass everyone said that the local Roman remains had been the palace of King Eveling and his daughter, the fairy Modron.

In Lanercost folk spoke in the 1880s of hearing the jingle of fairies' horses' harness, and 20 years later a Lanercost resident recalled a present of butter, left by fairies for a ploughman. One of his horses ate it and flourished; the other rejected it and died.

All Penrith knew of the 'Luck' of the Musgraves, of nearby Eden Hall. This was an ancient, elaborately decorated glass chalice. Antiquarians expressed varying opinions on its provenance, but the account preferred had nothing to do with scholarship.

It was said that on a summer night one of the hall's servants went to fetch water from St Cuthbert's Well, in the grounds. Nearby he saw fairies dancing around a glass beaker. Drawn to the goblet by its unusual design, he reached over the fairies and picked it up.

'If this cup should break or fall,' chanted the fairies, 'farewell the luck of Eden Hall.' So the chalice was thereafter kept carefully in a leather container. The hall's luck ran out in 1934, when the Musgraves' home was demolished. But the 'Luck' itself – identified as a 13th-century Syrian goblet, believed to have been acquired by a Musgrave during the Crusades – is preserved at the Victoria and Albert Museum.

Fairies could also be blamed when things went wrong. Thus, when bridge-building difficulties were encountered at Shap during the construction of the railway from Lancaster to Carlisle, fairies were convenient scapegoats. They could be relied upon to be elusive, like the one snapped by the Cumberland photographer

W.B. Redmayne when he spotted it while birdwatching near Dalston. On developing his film he was dismayed to find that the sprite was nowhere to be seen. . . .

Yet another vanishing act was performed on Souther Fell, near Threlkeld. And this time it wasn't just a few fairies that disappeared. It was a whole army.

On Midsummer Eve in 1735, a farm servant, Daniel Stricket, was astonished to see troops marching across Souther Fell. They appeared to be well-disciplined, and for an hour he watched company after company pass across the fell and disappear over the top. Few believed his story . . . until, two years later, again on Midsummer Eve, the spectacle was repeated. The army was on horseback, and this time it was witnessed by Stricket's employer, William Lancaster, and his family.

In 1743 a Wilton Hill farmer and one of his workers reported seeing a man and a dog on Souther Fell, chasing some horses. This didn't strike them as particularly unusual . . . until the man, dog and horses all vanished without a sound, over a precipice. A search of the fell beneath the cliff failed to find any bodies.

All this, however, was merely a curtain-raiser for what was to follow. On Midsummer Eve in 1745, the phantom army returned, its ranks interspersed this time with what appeared to be carriages, passing across terrain which was quite inaccessible to wheeled transport. The spectators on this occasion numbered some 26 witnesses, several of whom scoured the fell the next day for horseshoes, wheel-tracks and footprints, but found nothing. Yet they all knew what they had seen, saying they were prepared to swear to it before a magistrate; and 40 years later two survivors among them put their names to an attestation of what they had witnessed.

Those seeking a rational explanation spoke of mirages, of tricks performed by refractions of light – it was said that at the time of the 1745 illusion, rebel troops had been exercising on the south-west coast of Scotland. Others pointed out that Bonnie Prince Charlie didn't raise his standard until 19th August. They also noted that residents of the Souther Fell area had a reputation for credulity – there was a tradition that the reflection of stars could be seen at noon in the waters of Scales and Bowscale tarns, the latter being inhabited by two immortal fish.

Daniel Stricket, the first person to see the vanishing army, later became an auctioneer. Doubtless he pronounced 'Going, going, gone,' with rare conviction.

Lost in a Blizzard

THE knock at the door of George Rowlandson's Easedale home near Grasmere came at about noon on Monday, 21st March 1808. On the doorstep was one of the boys from the Greens' smallholding nearby. He asked if he could borrow a cloak. What did he want it for? asked Rowlandson. For his sister, the boy replied, so that she could go to look for their parents.

Where were they? The boy didn't know. They had gone over the fells to Langdale on Saturday afternoon to attend a furniture sale, and they hadn't returned.

Questioning the boy further, Rowlandson learned that George and Sarah Green had also intended to visit one of their daughters who was in service in Langdale, at the same time seeing her mistress to settle details of the girl's continuing employment.

Further inquiries were to confirm that the Greens had been at the sale, had called on their daughter and had then set off over the fells for home, leaving at about 5 pm. Then there had been a snowstorm.

Meanwhile, six of the couple's other children, the eldest a girl of eleven, the youngest a baby, had waited at home, sitting up until eleven o'clock on the Saturday

44

night. Then they had gone to bed, assuming their parents had decided to spend the night in Langdale because of the snow. Sunday had come and gone with still no sign of them. So now, the boy concluded, could he please borrow a cloak for his sister?

Rowlandson immediately set out to alert the men of the valley, a search party was formed and the fells were scoured along the route the Greens would have taken. George was 66, his wife 43, and there was no trace of them, although a shepherd recalled having seen two sets of footprints close together in the snow on the Sunday morning on the summit of Blea Crag, overlooking Easedale Tarn.

Little or no work was done in the valley on Tuesday. All able-bodied men were up in the fells as the search continued, but it was not until Wednesday afternoon that the couple were found. Sarah Green's body lay near Mill Beck, above Great Langdale, not far from Dungeon Ghyll. Searchers had previously been within feet of her, but she had been covered by snow. Her husband, his skull smashed, lay at the foot of a precipice nearby. In the blizzard which had overtaken them, visibility would have been nil. It was deduced that Sarah had been at George's side when he fell, for one of her shoes was found near the top of the cliff. Her badly bruised body indicated that she had fallen from another crag and had rolled down the fellside.

Two people in Langdale recalled having heard cries at about 10 pm on the Saturday night. Taken to be the shouts of drunks carousing after the sale, the calls had been ignored.

As soon as news had spread that the Greens were missing, women of the valley had hastened to look after the children. Now that their parents' death was confirmed, what was to be done with them? The tragedy was made worse by the family's financial plight. The Greens' home was the poorest in the valley, and although they owned it together with a cow and a patch of land, the property was heavily mortgaged. The way things had been going, it seemed as if the Greens would soon have had to part with it.

Writing at the time, William Wordsworth's sister Dorothy recorded: 'The cow was grown old, and they had not money to buy another. They had sold their horse, and were in the habit of carrying any trifles they could spare out of the house or stable to barter for potatoes or meal. Luxuries they had none. They never made tea, and when the neighbours went to look after the children they found nothing in the house but two boilings of potatoes, a very little meal, a little bread, and three or four legs of lean dried mutton. The cow at that time did not give a quart of milk in the day.

'You will wonder how they lived at all, and indeed I can scarcely tell you. They used to sell a few peats in the summer, which they dug out of their own hearts' heart, their land. The old man might earn a little money by doing jobs for his neighbours, but it was not known till now (at least by us) how much distressed they must have been, for they were never heard to murmur or complain.'

In fact they had always seemed cheerful and had always dressed decently when visiting a friend or a sale, Dorothy Wordsworth noted. 'Alas! a love of Sales had always been their failing, being perhaps the only publick meetings in this neighbourhood where social pleasure is to be had without the necessity of expending money . . .

Perhaps formerly it might be said, and with truth, that the Woman had better been at home; but who shall assert that this same spirit which led her to come at times among her Neighbours as an equal, seeking like them society and pleasure, that this spirit did not assist greatly in preserving her in chearful independance of mind through the many hardships and privations of extreme poverty?'

Visiting the orphans with her sister-in-law shortly before their parents were found, Dorothy remarked that the children, although ragged, were always clean. None seemed unhealthy, 'except the youngest, a fair and beautiful Infant. It looks sickly, but not suffering; there is a heavenly patience in its countenance, and while it lay asleep in its cradle three days after its Mother's death, one could not look upon it without fanciful thoughts that the Babe had been sent into this life but to be her Companion, and was ready to follow in tranquil peace.'

But little Hannah Green was to live well into her eighties.

Dorothy was at the Greens' home again for the couple's funeral. 'The furniture of the house was decayed and scanty,' she noted. 'But there was one oaken Cupboard that was so bright with rubbing that it was plain it had been prized as an ornament and a treasure by the poor Woman then lying in her coffin.'

Before the bodies were removed for the funeral procession, a threepenny loaf of bread was handed to each of the mourners. Mary Wordsworth, William's wife, was loth to accept hers, thinking the orphans were in no state to give anything away; then she had second thoughts. The handing out of bread on such occasions was, after all, a time-honoured local custom which the children had thought should be observed. It was not the first bereavement their home had seen.

In Grasmere church, Dorothy recorded, 'the two Coffins were placed near the Altar, and the whole Family knelt on the floor on each side of the Father's Coffin, leaning over it. The eldest Daughter had been unable to follow with the rest of the Mourners, and we had led her back to the house before she got through the first field; the second fainted by the Graveside; and their Brother stood like a Statue of Despair silent and motionless; the younger Girls sobbed aloud. Many tears were shed by persons who had known little of the Deceased; and all the people who were gathered together appeared to be united in one general feeling of sympathy for the hopeless condition of the Orphans.'

After the funeral the family returned to their home, where the furniture was sold on the following Thursday, leaving the cottage empty and deserted. But as soon as the church service ended, an Ambleside woman had taken four of the Green boys to live at her home pending whatever arrangements might be made for them and stop-gap accommodation for the others was also arranged. A committee of six women was formed to oversee the children's future and to manage a subscription fund which had been launched for their upkeep, and within a month homes for all the orphans had been found in the neighbourhood.

Two dukes and six lords were among those who responded to the appeal, which raised just over £500 and was finally closed upon William Wordsworth's recommendation that were the fund to amount to more it might unsettle the orphans by elevating them above their station. The greater part of the money was invested, and when the trust was finally wound up in 1829 each orphan – by now grown up – was presented with £60.

The Greens' story drew a poem from Wordsworth and accounts from authors including Thomas de Quincey and Charlotte M. Yonge. But although friends pressed Dorothy Wordsworth to publish her own more intimate memoir, she declined to do so until 30 or 40 years had elapsed, 'when the characters of the children are formed and they can be no longer objects of curiosity'.

The
Art of Lying

WILL RITSON, a champion wrestler, farmer and the first landlord of what is now the Wasdale Head Hotel, was celebrated as a teller of tall stories. He was also a story in himself, in a valley with no shortage of tales. Wasdale, it was said, had the deepest lake, highest mountain, smallest church and biggest liar in all England.

Most of those claims were true, although Wasdale's possession of the nation's tiniest church was disputed. Nevertheless it was here that the congregation was once treated to a spectacle that must surely have been peculiar to this valley. When the bell-ringer lent the bell-rope to a farmer to tie up his hay cart, and the rope was not returned in time for Sunday service, the ringer simply straddled the roof of the low-built church and rang the bell with a hammer. Or so Will Ritson said.

By the time of his retirement from the hotel in 1879 he was almost as well known as Wastwater itself. He had his own pack of foxhounds, and his circle had included Wordsworth, de Quincey, 'Christopher North' of *Black-wood's Magazine*, celebrated mountaineers and numerous professors. When Princess Louise and her retinue arrived via Sty Head Pass to pay him a call, stampeding sheep as they descended, he declared the princess to be 'a gay canny body, for she's browt her mutton wi' her'.

He had no high opinion, however, of Londoners. Asked why the stream behind his home had such large trout, he said this was due to 'those fwoak frae Lunnon'. They arrived lousy as sheep, had a dip in the beck, and the fish fed from what was washed off them.

On another occasion a visitor remarked, 'Fancy living here all your life. Why don't you come up to London and see the sights?' There was no call for Wasdale folk to go sightseeing in London, the innkeeper replied, because some of the sights of London 'coom doon here t' see us'.

He told of a turnip that was so large that a bullock was lost after eating its way into it, and he recalled a tall haystack built by a Nether Wasdale farmer and his lad. When the stack was completed, the boy called from the top, 'Mester, hoo is Ah to git doon?'

'Shut thi een an' walk aboot a bit,' the farmer replied.

There were times, however, when Ritson's reputation for tall stories became irksome as he was repeatedly pressed to perform. 'Reet,' he told one persistent guest, 'thoo wants a greet lee. Ah'll tell thi th' biggest lee Ah's ivver tell't. Thoo's t' handsomest feller Ah've ivver seen.'

The clergy were frequent victims. After accompanying a parson to a mountain top, he told him he was now as near to heaven as he'd ever get. And it was to a bishop that he yielded his title as champion liar, when the prelate announced he had never told a lie in his life.

Anyone attempting to pull the hotelier's leg invariably came off worst, as when a tourist invited him to admire the view through his telescope, trained from the summit of Scafell onto a church in Keswick.

'If you look steadily at the vane,' said the visitor, 'you'll see a fly on it.'

But there were no flies on Will Ritson. 'Aye, aye,' he replied, taking a squint. 'An' it's a pied [one-eyed] yan!'

It was in a sombre mood, however, that he told a group of women visitors about six children and their parents who had been caught in a cloudburst while negotiating Sty Head Pass. Desperate to reach their home, they waded into the resulting torrent, were swept away and perished.

Silence prevailed as he concluded the account and his guests pondered the tragedy.

'Ah weel, it might ha' bin worse,' the innkeeper reflected.

'Worse?' cried one of the listeners.

'Aye. It might ha' bin true.'

Today Wasdale's tradition of telling tall stories is perpetuated at the Bridge Inn at the bottom end of the valley, where an annual contest is held much like the one in the last century which Will Ritson entered, but from which he asked to withdraw when it came to his turn.

Asked why, he confessed that he could not tell a lie – and was declared the outright winner.

A
Cumbrian Abroad

WHEN a wife is described as having been 'of admirable fortitude and patience', one assumes she had a difficult husband. But John Woodcock Graves was more than difficult. He was impossible. Yet 'impossible' people are often talented. Graves died in obscurity, few having heard of him. But he made one of his friends a household name when in 1832 he wrote a song 'for my darling daughters and the errand boy'. It was *D'Ye Ken John Peel?*

The huntsman thus immortalised was by no means as extraordinary, however, as his chronicler. John Woodcock Graves was born in 1795 at Wigton, the son of a glazier. Although he received little education, he became interested in mathematics, mechanics and drawing and he was inventive by nature.

Within a year of his marriage at 21 he was a widower. A few years later he married Abigail Porthouse, who was to need every ounce of the patience and fortitude ascribed to her.

The couple settled at Caldbeck, also the home of John Peel, who was to be buried there in 1854. Graves, a weaver, established a wool factory which flourished and doubtless would have continued to do so, had he not received a visit from the man who was to become Lord Brougham. Aware of Graves' ingenuity in mechanics and his reputation as a would-be entrepreneur, Brougham persuaded him to invest in a coal mine.

The weaver then began to lose interest in Caldbeck Mill. Noted for his violent temper, he came to blows with his mill's manager, found himself in court and decided he'd had enough of Caldbeck. He went to London, where he quickly decided to make a fresh start in the convict settlement of Van Diemen's Land – subsequently Tasmania – where land was available for the asking.

In Caldbeck his wife received a message telling her to settle any debts and to pack and join him. When she demurred, another message came telling her that he was going and their children were sailing with him, whether she liked it or not. So Abigail reluctantly packed, and with their two sons and two daughters she arrived with her husband in Hobart in 1833.

Graves didn't make a good settler. He hadn't the temperament to settle anywhere, and his mood wasn't improved by a succession of misfortunes. On their first night in Hobart, the family's possessions were stolen by convicts. Graves couldn't get a job, his attempts at self-employment were unsuccessful and he felt he had been cheated by the Government which hadn't granted him as many acres of free land as he claimed he'd been led to expect.

The violence of the threats he began making against the authorities convinced them that he was mad, and he was put in a lunatic asylum. But his ingenuity hadn't deserted him. Finding a kindred spirit in a visiting magistrate, another devotee of hunting, he asked for paint and brushes so that he might produce a mural around the asylum yard depicting a kangaroo hunt led by the magistrate.

The materials were provided and Graves set to work. His picture took shape and at last the time came for him to fill in the sky. For this he needed a ladder, so one was supplied. The artist's work continued until, with his final brush-stroke of vivid blue, he dropped over the wall to freedom and disappeared.

Three years passed before his family heard from him. In that time he went to New Zealand and Sydney, but when he found they suited him no better than Hobart he returned to berate his long-suffering wife for breaking up their home.

In his absence Abigail had done her best to support herself and the children by taking in washing, doing sewing and discovering a latent talent for teaching, for she was well educated. One of the daughters had been adopted by the Bishop of Tasmania, and her sister had become a governess; one of the sons had become articled to a lawyer, while his brother had found work as a shipwright and was later to become a successful timber-merchant.

Following Abigail's death, John Woodcock Graves continued to come, go and do as he pleased, regardless of anyone else. So long as he had some kind of a roof over his head, his books, mathematical instruments and whatever mechanical apparatus he was designing to hand, he was as content as he would ever be. And, despite everything, his children continued to do what they could for him, regarding their father with an exasperated affection.

First they suggested that the old man should live near Melbourne with his timber-merchant son and grand-children. No, he said, the climate there was too hot for him, and he would only be an encumbrance. Finally he agreed to his children buying him a cottage and installing a housekeeper.

Knowing his father, however, the timber-merchant guessed the arrangement wouldn't work – 'If he had a house at the top of Mount Wellington he would want it at the bottom; if he had it at the bottom he would want it at the top; if at the east he would want it at the west.'

And so it turned out. Allowing his new home to become a shambles, Graves left it and went to live in a slum, protesting that the gradient to the cottage had become too much for him. Now he wanted his home to be sold so that he could spend the proceeds on another scheme stemming from one of his inventions.

When he became ill, a daughter, already all but bankrupted by the cottage experiment, went to look after him, but he didn't want her around. 'He thought I would interfere with his freedom,' she later recorded, 'as I generally kept him in good trim when I was mistress of the house ... long before I was tired of my visit he would ask me repeatedly when I was going home. To the last he was sternly independent, proud as Lucifer and just as violent as ever he was when a young man.'

A few years before his death at 91 in 1886, Graves told how his celebrated song came to be written. He had penned it, he recorded, while sitting with John Peel in a snug parlour in Caldbeck: 'We were then both of us in the heyday of manhood, and hunters of the older fashion, meeting the night before to arrange earth-stopping, and in the morning to take the best part of the

56

hunt – the drag over the mountains in the mist – while fashionable hunters still lay in the blankets.

'Large flakes of snow fell that evening. We sat by the fireside, hunting over again many a good run and recalling the feats of each particular hound, or narrow neck-breck 'scapes, when a flaxen-haired daughter of mine came in saying, "Father, what do they say to what Granny sings?"

'Granny was singing to sleep my eldest son – now a leading barrister in Hobart Town – with an old rant called "Bonnie Annie". The pen and ink for hunting appointments lay on the table. The idea of writing a song to this old air forced itself upon me, and thus was produced impromptu "D'Ye Ken John Peel?"

'Immediately after, I sung it to poor Peel, who smiled through a stream of tears which fell down his manly cheeks, and I well remember saying to him, in a joking style, "By Jove, Peel, you'll be sung when we're both run to earth." '

The Terrible
Knitters of Dent

FEW people today would fancy walking 39 miles from the far side of Dent, near Sedbergh, to Langdale. Fewer still would contemplate such a tramp in snow. And nobody at all would think such a hike possible by two little girls. Betty Yewdale was seven and her sister Sally two years her junior. They walked those 39 miles. In snow, by themselves, on 18th-century unsurfaced roads. And nearly 70 years were to pass before their story was told.

Wordsworth apparently first met Betty Yewdale by chance. She was then middle-aged, living with her handsome but somewhat slow-witted husband Jonathan at High Hacket, on the fells above Little Langdale. He was a quarryman, she helped with their smallholding, and they had no children. According to Wordsworth's *The Excursion*, his initial encounter with Betty Yewdale occurred when, half-lost on the fells when darkness overtook him, he saw a light on the hillside. It shone at a spot which seemed too high for habitation, but as he had nothing else to guide him he headed in its direction. It turned out to be a lantern held by a woman waiting to lead her husband home after his day's work at a Little

Langdale quarry.

The woman was Betty, who in the poem shows the author to a seat at her fireside and then goes out again with her lantern to resume her watch for her husband. A friendship apparently developed, for in 1810 it was to the bracing air of High Hacket that Wordsworth's children were sent from Grasmere to recover from whooping cough.

Robert Southey, who lived in Keswick and in 1813 became poet laureate, was curious about the woman portrayed in *The Excursion* and asked his daughter and Wordsworth's wife's sister to go to see her. Betty Yewdale was by then in her old age, living in a cottage at Rydal. But her memory was unimpaired and she had an unusual childhood story to tell, in the broadest dialect. Her visitors were beguiled both by her tale and her speech. They wrote down her story just as she told it, gave it to Southey, and in 1847 it was published in the second part of his miscellany *The Doctor*.

Betty's father had a smallholding in Langdale. He also had more daughters than were needed at home. So when a woman visiting the valley from Dent offered to take two of the girls back with her and teach them the knitting trade, the parents thought it a good idea.

A financial arrangement was agreed, and without more ado Betty and her five-year-old sister were despatched, Betty sharing a horse with a man accompanying the woman, who on her own horse perched Sally in front of her.

They were 'terrible knitters' in Dent, Betty Yewdale recalled 65 years later, meaning they were terribly good at it. But the sisters didn't like Dent at all. It wasn't that they were mistreated, just that they were homesick and couldn't stand the food. They were also overwhelmed by so much knitting. At a school about a mile away 'we o' knit as hard as we cud drive,' striving to see which 'cud knit hardest yan again anudder.'

Their day's work was allotted them before they set off each morning and if they didn't complete it 'we warrant to gang to our dinners – they hed o' macks [had all kinds] o' contrivances to larn us to knit swift.' Those who knitted slowest 'raffled tudders' yarn an' geet weel thumpt'.

Christmas came, and all the sisters could think of was how to get back to Langdale – 'neet an' day ther was nought but this knitting.' They knitted stockings, gloves, night caps, waistcoats and petticoats, and when Betty completed a stocking in six hours, Sally knitting one in seven, their employer sent a note to their parents to tell them.

'Sally an' me, when we were by oursells, were always contrivin' how we were at git away. When we sleept by oursells we talk't of nought else, but when t'woman's doughter sleept wi' us we were quite mum. Summat or udder always happent at hinder us till yan day, between Kursmas an' Cannalmas [Candlemas], when t'woman's doughter stait at heaam, we teuk off. Our house was four mile on t'odder side o' Dent's Town whor, efter we hed pass t'skeul, we axed t'way to Kendal.'

There was snow on the ground but it was beginning to thaw and was 'varra sloshy an' cauld … we hed our clogs on for we dursn't change them for our shoon for fear o' being fund out, an' we hed nought on but our hats, an' bits o' blue bedgowns an' brats [aprons]. I hed a sixpence e' my pocket, an' we hed three or four shillings mare in our box, 'at our fwoak hed ge'en us to keep our pocket wi'. But, lile mafflins [little perplexed ones] as we were, we thought it wad be misst an' dursn't tak ony mare.'

Before they got to Sedbergh they became hungry, so they went to a large house just off the road and begged for a bit of bread, but were turned away. Tramping on, they reached another house, where Betty told her little sister to do the begging this time as she was the smallest and stood a better chance of success. It worked, and they were given a large slice of bread.

Then they arrived at 'Scotch Jins, as they ca' t' public house about three mile fra Sebber [Sedbergh] o' this side – a Scotch woman keept it.' As it was almost dark they asked the landlady to let them stay the night. She took them in, gave them some boiled milk and bread and put them to bed. 'We tel't her our taael an' she sed we were in t' reet at run away.'

The next morning they gave her their sixpence and went on their way, crossing a cold moor in rain and begging at another house at Hay Fell where they found a woman 'an' a heap o' raggelty bairns' standing round a table, where the mother gave them some porridge and some sugar in a cup of cold tea.

At Peat Lane turnpike gate they were taken in, allowed to warm themselves, were given bread and were told they had done right to run away 'for Dent was t' poorest place in t' warld'.

It was nearly dark when they reached Kendal, where they asked a woman the way to 'Tom Post's'. He was the man who took letters from Kendal to Ambleside and Hawkshead once a week, and the sisters remembered eating at his home during a visit from Langdale to Kendal. The woman gave them directions and they set off, but on looking back they saw she was standing watching them. She then approached them, questioned them, and took them to her home by the bridge they had crossed on entering the town. Hers was a very poor house with no fire, but she fetched some kindling and peat and lit one. Then she sought out some of her clothes and tied them round the children as best she could, putting their own wet garments to dry in front of the fire.

After making them some tea, she told them she'd no bed for them in her house, but she took them to a neighbour's. There they shared a bedroom with an old woman who had a fit in the night, her face turning black as coal. People came in and stood round her.

'We heeard them say 'at we were asleep, sea we meade as if we were, because we thought if we were asleep they waddn't kill us. An' we wisht oursells e' t' streets again or onny whor, an' wad ha' been fain to ha' been ligging under a dyke [would rather have been lying in a ditch].'

The next morning they had breakfast and the woman who had befriended them gave them each a ha'penny cake to eat as they continued their journey, accompanying them to the top of the House of Correction hill. Now it was freezing, the road was slippery and they made slow progress to Staveley. Hungry again, they began to eat their cakes, deciding to walk so far, take a bit, walk so far again, and then take another. The cakes had gone by the time they reached Ings chapel. Every now and then as they continued they would stop for a rest, weeping as they sat in the shelter of a wall, cuddled together.

It was dark before they reached Ambleside, and as

they rounded the top of Lake Windermere the waves sounded so melancholy that they sat down on a stone and had another cry. Trudging on through Clappers-gate, they felt better on a road that was familiar and realised that folk there would know them should they call for food and shelter. Uppermost in their minds now, however, was the fear that their parents would be angry with them for running away.

At last, at two in the morning, they reached their own door.

'I ca'ed out "Fadder! Fadder! Mudder! Mudder!" ower an' ower again,' Betty recalled. 'She hard us, an' sed, "That's our Betty's voice."

' "Thou's nought but fancies, lig still," sed my fadder, but she waddent. She gat up an' opent duir and there warr we stanning doddering an' daized wi' cauld, as neer dead as macks nea matter. When she so us she was mare flate [frightened] than we. She brast out a-crying, an' we grat [wept], an' my fadder grat an a'. An' they duddent flight [scold] nor say nought tull us for cumming away. They warrant a bit angert, an' my fadder sed we warrant nivver gang back again.'

The sisters' employers in Dent had not missed them until nightfall, thinking the two had been kept back to finish their tasks. Then searchers set out for Kendal, passing 'Scotch Jins' where the girls were sleeping, and finally abandoning the chase when there was no sign of them and it was assumed the sisters had gone home.

'My fadder wasn't lang, ye may be seur, finding out t'woman at Kendal 'at was sea good tull us,' said Betty. 'My mudder put her down a pot o' butter an' meead her a lile cheese an' sent her.'

A
Curious Caller

MITERDALE is one of the Lake District's least-
known valleys. Some guidebooks neglect it
altogether, and its legend has often been ascribed to
Eskdale Green, where the ruins of a farmhouse have
been pointed out with the words, 'That's where it
happened.' But it didn't. It happened in Miterdale.

The valley is small, as its river Mite suggests, and it
was part of a packhorse route in the days when it still
had an inn; and a farm at Miterdale Head, where one
morning the farmer set off to market for the day, telling
his wife that he might be away overnight and reminding
her to lock up in his absence.

As dusk began to fall the farmer's wife busied herself
making tallow candles, looking up every now and then
to see if she could catch a glimpse of her husband
returning up the dale. But there was no sign of him.
Another figure appeared in the gloom, however, making
its way down from Burnmoor.

As the person drew nearer the farmer's wife saw it was
a woman, wearing a scarf to shield her head. Knocking
at the door, the caller said she had lost her way. Could
the farmer's wife put her up for the night?

The wife didn't like the look of her, but the woman was clearly weary and haggard, so she was shown in and given a seat by the fire. The farmer's wife put her candle-making to one side and began to prepare a meal.

At the fireside, the stranger began to nod off. Her head drooped and her scarf fell to the floor as she dozed. She was fast asleep when the farmer's wife turned to tell her the meal was about to be served ... and saw that this was no woman at her fireside. The slumbering visitor was a villainous-looking man.

The farmer's wife froze, her mind racing. What would the man do when he awoke to find that his scarf had slipped off, betraying his disguise? And why was he dressed as a woman? To trick his way into the house, of course, where she was alone with her baby, thought the farmer's wife. He'd come to rob and murder them.

She must act quickly, she decided, before the man stirred. The boiling sheep fat she had been using to make candles was to hand. The man in the fireside chair now had his head back, his mouth wide open. She picked up a ladle, scooped up some scalding tallow, and poured it down his throat. Another ladle followed.

Her husband returned the following morning to find his wife hysterical. On the floor lay the man in woman's clothes, choked to death by the tallow. Without more ado, the farmer buried the body on his land, saying nothing of what had happened until many years later.

The story subsequently found its way into Alice Rea's *Beckside Boggles*, but it was not until the 1960s that the mystery of the man dressed as a woman was perhaps explained. It was then that the Cumbrian writer Dudley Hoys noted the discovery of an ancient local newspaper containing an account of a murder in Whitehaven. Two seamen had quarrelled on the quay, one stabbing the other to death, and the killer had taken to the fells. Subsequently, a lonely farmhouse had been broken into during the owner's absence, and some of the farmer's wife's clothes had been stolen. . . .

Miracles
by Order

C OVERING about 14 acres, Great Urswick Tarn is rust-coloured because of iron ore sediment brought down by Clerk's Beck from the Lindale mines. But one 18th-century account of the tarn is even more colourful.

This maintained that those tawny waters conceal the market town of Lile Ooston, a busier place than Kendal or Lancaster in its day. All it lacked was a convenient water supply, and the town's women became tired of drawing from wells to replenish the limestone troughs for their cattle. They consequently gave their priest an ultimatum: if he didn't do something about the water shortage, they would stop attending his services.

The priest accordingly performed a ritual involving thunder, lightning and a cloudburst which created Clerk's Beck and solved the water problem. Then the stream began to acquire its iron ore tinge, and the women of Lile Ooston weren't having that. The priest was summoned again.

He cautioned them that he might not be able to control a further miraculous inundation. If anything went wrong, he warned, it would be their responsibility.

The women told him to get on with it.

A further ritual was enacted. From the churchyard which overlooks the tarn today the priest called forth a storm which swiftly got out of hand and created the pool which now covers Lile Ooston.

A rival account claimed that the tarn was the result of an earthquake provoked by the wickedness of the local witches, partial to transforming men into pigs and dogs whenever the fancy took them. All this reflects badly on the women of Great Urswick, but perhaps it was a village of misogynists.

It was also claimed that the tarn was bottomless and could not be fathomed, a myth dispelled in 1853 by an Urswick man who was nothing if not practical. Taking advantage of a severe winter, he bored through the tarn's thick ice and took soundings which established an average depth of 39 feet. But I doubt if this made him popular.

He also claimed that the tarn would eventually be so silted up by iron ore sediment that it would disappear, becoming a meadow crossed by Clerk's Beck. This notion was prompted by his observation that while the tarn's inlet carried the all-too-visible stain, the waters of the outlet were clear. However, he assured villagers that the tarn would endure for their lifetime. The rate at which sediment was deposited – half an inch annually – meant that the tarn would survive for 923 years. What he couldn't foresee was that his calculations would be upset in the early 1970s when Gleaston Beck was cleared and the level of the tarn promptly dropped 12 inches.

Time was when Great Urswick also had a communal knife, supposedly the only such implement in the parish. This was always kept stuck in the bark of a particular tree so that anyone needing it knew where to find it. If it was being used, whoever wanted it next stood by the tree and cried 'Whittle here!'

One day a villager arrived at the tree to find the knife absent. Then a second person needing the knife arrived to take up the cry, followed by yet another. Before long two thirds of the parish had gathered, shouting in unison. Who had last been seen with the knife? The village idiot. He was accordingly sought out and confirmed that he'd had it. When he had finished with it he had been far from the tree and short of time. He had therefore buried the knife at a well-marked spot until he could return it to its accustomed place. It would be easy to find. The spot was in a ploughed field, he explained, just where a small cloud had cast its shadow.

Finsthwaite's Princess

HAD you strolled around Rydal in the early 1940s you might have seen Queen Wilhemina of the Netherlands cycling off to do her shopping in Ambleside. Her wartime residence was Rydal Hall and everyone knew who she was, which is more than can be said of Clementina Johannes Sobieski Douglass, otherwise known as the Finsthwaite Princess. Nobody's quite sure about her to this day.

She is said to have come to the village as a child in 1745, living at Waterside House with two servants. On her death there in 1771 – according to tradition – she requested an unmarked grave with no tombstone or epitaph. There she lay in anonymity in the village churchyard until 1913 when a plain cross was erected bearing her name, taken from the parish register. And what a name! Genealogists had a field day.

Johannes Sobieski III was King of Poland. His granddaughter Clementina was the mother of Charles Edward Stuart, who used the name Douglass when travelling incognito. Another Clementina was the Young Pretender's mistress. Small wonder that many see the Finsthwaite woman's name as a signpost to her origin.

They say she must have been Bonnie Prince Charlie's illegitimate daughter. And they quote an account of 1899 which recalled that the old folk of the village always referred to Clementina as 'the princess'.

Nonsense, say sceptics. The woman was a recluse and such people often inspire fanciful stories. She was more probably mentally retarded and was sent to live in seclusion at Finsthwaite to spare her parents embarrassment. Furthermore, Prince Charles Edward had only one known illegitimate daughter, who became the Duchess of Albany, and he claimed she was his only child.

Fathers, however, are not noted for their keenness to acknowledge illegitimate children and revealing the infant Clementina's existence at a time of rebellion would have endangered the child's safety.

Others point to the fact that Waterside House was owned by a Catholic family which had Jacobite connections. That would have made the place an ideal retreat for the Young Pretender's daughter in the fateful year of 1745. And if Clementina were retarded, what was she doing in 1770 witnessing the will of a Finsthwaite landowner?

There is also a tradition that Clementina's possessions included a medal commemorating the marriage of the Old Pretender and Princess Clementina Sobieski. She is said to have bequeathed this to a Finsthwaite friend, a Miss Penny. If such a medal existed, it has long since vanished.

All that can be said with probability is that Finsthwaite's 'princess' had a Stuart and Polish royal family connection. Until whatever that relationship was is revealed, the enigma will endure as Cumbria's equivalent of such controversies as the identity of Jack the Ripper and of the dark lady of Shakespeare's sonnets. Whoever solves such mysteries will earn respect – but not popularity. They will have deprived us of endless pleasurable speculation.

Backing
a Loser

THERE was no doubt about it, the British authorities decided. Count Ferdinand von Zeppelin was onto something. His first airship had been launched in 1900, and its military potential was obvious. Britain must have one. The £28,000 contract was awarded to Vickers at Barrow-in-Furness. The company was to build an airship in collaboration with the Royal Navy.

Envisaging a lucrative future in the skies, Vickers at their own expense erected a vast shed for the project at Cavendish Dock. In return for this commitment the Government had assured the company that all airship work would be theirs for at least ten years.

The deal was struck in 1908 and by May 1911 all was just about ready. But not quite. For when His Majesty's Airship No 1 was eased out of the shed for trials it became apparent that it was too heavy to achieve lift-off, so back it went into the workshop for modification. Three weeks earlier, newspapers had reported the crash at Aldershot of a smaller airship which had become Britain's first when it made its maiden flight of 30 miles from London's Crystal Palace in 1902....

By now Barrow's cynics had christened the town's airship the Mayfly – it may fly, or it may not. But all eyes were ready to scan the sky on 22nd September 1911, when the silver and yellow monster emerged from its shed again, poised perfectly some 20 feet above the water.

Photographers had set up their cameras on tripods to record the event, and it was just as well they were ready. The airship had hardly appeared before it was caught by a sudden gust of wind and heeled over on its beam ends. It slowly righted itself, but as its crew swung it round to head back to Cavendish Dock there was a rending sound. The Mayfly's back had broken, and as it settled on the water the crew in the rear gondola became perhaps the first ever to abandon airship. The Mayfly's tail, freed of its weight, rose high above the water and the airship broke in two.

Altogether the venture had cost more than £40,000, but Vickers did not give up. In 1915 a successor to the Mayfly made its maiden flight over Barrow and two more followed, one being used as flagship when German submarines surrendered off Harwich in 1918, the other becoming celebrated in 1919 for remaining airborne for 40 hours. Work had already begun on constructing a new streamlined airship, the R80. This was built at Vickers' Walney Island sheds under the supervision of its designer Barnes Wallis, of subsequent *Dambusters* renown. It was to be the last airship produced at Barrow.

The next time the town saw one was in 1936 when the Hindenburg passed over twice. It was reported to have photographed the works where Vickers had meanwhile returned to doing what they knew best. In

BACKING A LOSER

1901 they had produced the first submarines commissioned by the Royal Navy, beginning an association that has continued to this day.

Going All Out

MENTION 'Miss England' today and most people think of beauty queens. More than 60 years ago there was a very different Miss England, also a beauty. She was well-known in Windermere, where she came to grief, watched by thousands. To be precise, she wasn't simply Miss England – she was Miss England II, the boat in which Sir Henry Segrave planned to exceed everyone else's speed on water.

Nowadays, attempts on the world water speed record conjure up pictures of a lone hero in the cockpit. It was different in 1930. Miss England II had a crew of three … and I spent a fair chunk of my childhood in the company of their sole survivor – Michael 'Jack' Willcocks, who was Segrave's engineer.

Twenty-five years ago, I asked him what it was like on 13th June 1930. What went wrong? Was anyone to blame? This is his story.

It was eggs for breakfast – scrambled eggs, he recalled – at Bowness's Old England Hotel where he had slept well in the annexe. Not the troubled sleep you might expect of somebody about to risk his life. He had been only too glad to turn in at ten the previous evening, exhausted by his journey from Saunders Roe's Isle of Wight shipyard in a solid-tyred lorry, jolting over setts and cobblestones for much of the way through the Midlands.

'It was the most uncomfortable ride of my life. So wearying that I got out of the cab and into Miss England on the back of the lorry, doing my best to have a nap on the cockpit floor under the tarpaulin. But sleep was impossible.'

It had all started with an invitation to meet Segrave, who, having become the fastest man on land, now wished to achieve the same feat on water. Michael Willcocks's engineering background, war service in Royal Navy coastal motor boats and experience of racing a boat built to his own specification had made him a likely candidate for the post of Miss England II's engineer. What Segrave particularly required was someone able to improvise replacement parts if things went wrong, and Willcocks had that ability.

It would be no joy ride, Sir Henry had warned. If there were a mishap it was unlikely that any of the crew would survive. 'We are going all out, and if you decide to come I will expect you to stay with the job whatever happens. So I won't take your decision now. Go home and think about it for a week.'

'And that', Michael Willcocks told me, 'was the worst week I ever spent – worrying whether I was good enough for the job.'

Rising at seven o'clock on the 13th, he was down at the slipway at eight. 'Don't forget the date, Wilkie!' shouted Miss England's propeller-manufacturer.

'Friday the 13th is my lucky day,' said Willcocks.

The typewritten notice issued the previous day to each member of the team announced: 'Miss England II will attempt the record tomorrow afternoon at 4 pm. She will run between the pylons on the West or Lancashire shore of the Lake and within one hundred yards of the buoys...'

The weather was perfect. A shortage of propellers – they kept breaking under stress – had at last been overcome. But the armoured jackets being made to order for the attempt had not arrived. In retrospect, Willcocks was to think that things might have turned out differently if they had – 'but I hadn't the slightest physical worry because I had such faith in Segrave. And anyway I hadn't time to be frightened. I was too busy.'

At 1.15 the four-and-a-half ton boat was towed out from her shed. Immensely strong, she had not been built for an attempt on the record but for racing, with a hull robust enough to withstand the combined wash of two other boats. A crew of at least two was necessary as there was too much for one to do – it would have been impossible for Segrave both to drive and attend to the engines. There were too many dials to watch, too many levers to pull. Michael Willcocks was also supposed to note down eight or nine readings every five seconds – 'but I never managed it.'

Also on board for the attempt was Vic Halliwell, a representative of Rolls-Royce, suppliers of the boat's 4,000 horsepower engines.

First Miss England raced north. Then south. A tap on the shoulder from Sir Henry and a thumbs up sign told Michael Willcocks they had broken the record – subject to confirmation. On shore, a national newspaper reporter phoned his office with an account of the successful attempt and left. What happened next got him the sack, and was the making of him, as I discovered years later when I met him in newspaper management.

Miss England II now wheeled around for what was to be the real test. Breaking the record had been well within the vessel's capacity. What the thousands lining the shores of Windermere didn't realise was that the establishment of a new record of 98.76 mph, which they had just witnessed, was only a curtain-raiser. With the United States world record broken and the propeller having withstood the stress, Segrave now proposed to see what Miss England II would do in excess of 120 mph.

As the boat streaked north, Willcocks noticed that Sir Henry was smiling. He also noted the engines' water temperature was rising, approaching the permitted maximum. He looked ahead to see how much further they had to go. Soon he would have to request a reduction in revs.

'Then there was a slight thud and the boat started to snake. Then she came up. I can remember thinking: she shouldn't do this. I was never more surprised in my life, because no boat should turn over when it's going straight ahead. Now the bows were rising and I could see we were going into the drink. You know how it used to be in the cinema when the film broke and you saw a lot of streaks. That's how the water looked to me. I drew my knees up to avoid being trapped in the boat. Getting to the surface was like scrambling up a greasy tube, and I couldn't see very well. Then I went down again and I began to see better. Vic Halliwell went by, buttocks up, bubbles coming from his overalls, and disappeared. Sir Henry went past in a series of jerks, and he disappeared. Then I was on the surface again and I could see boats. The boat of the Clerk of the Course was coming fast towards me. It had no clutches and no reverse, but by switching off it stopped just short of me – a splendid piece of handling. I'd just about had it – there was no wind in my body. Then Bob Coles, joint boss of the Windermere Motor Company, reached out and grabbed my hand...'

Meanwhile, a holidaymaker who had been photographing the attempt from his launch dived, fully clothed, into the lake to rescue Segrave. Taken to Belle Grange, a house on the Lancashire bank, Sir Henry had head injuries, both arms broken, two ribs fractured and a badly crushed thigh.

'How', he asked, 'are the lads?' Two and a half hours later he was still conscious. Then he suffered a haemorrhage due to a perforated lung. Two minutes later he was dead.

Halliwell's body had also been quickly recovered. He had been killed instantly, apparently breaking his neck on impact with the water.

To this day, nobody knows with certainty what went wrong, although Miss England is believed to have struck a log – a branch bearing three scratches was afterwards found floating nearby. Attempts to deduce the cause of the accident were not helped by souvenir hunters – one went off with what might have been a telltale piece of debris; another was seen carrying Miss England's Union Jack to the station.

Two days later, Michael Willcocks was out and about again despite a damaged spine, a massive bruise on his thigh and a knee-to-ankle gash on his left leg. 'For six weeks, the whites of my eyes were a vivid scarlet – the blood vessels in my eyeballs had burst when my goggles collapsed.'

When Miss England II was retrieved from nearly 200 feet of water a fortnight after the tragedy, he was there, taking part in the recovery and subsequently busying himself with the boat's renovation. But the smash was to cause him years of continuous pain and it left him with a limp – 'I fall over easily ... I have little or no feeling in my legs. Tickle my feet – no reaction.'

After Windermere, he went on to race in Italy and South America with Kaye Don, before becoming chairman of a light engineering firm in Somerset. He didn't see the Lake District again until the 1950s, when he came north for my wedding. The last time I saw him the demise of Donald Campbell, attempting to break his own 276.33 mph record on Coniston Water in 1967, was still fresh in everyone's minds. Michael Willcocks had watched the television coverage with particular interest – 'I felt that if only he could have completed the loop he would have been all right.'

A
Kitchen-boy
King

~~❧~~

YOU'RE too young to remember the German invasion. So am I. It was among the more bizarre events of 1487, and it took place in Cumbria. One morning, the residents of Ulverston awoke to find that 2,000 German soldiers were camped at Swarthmoor, just outside the town. How they came to be there is one of the area's strangest stories.

It began some months earlier. Henry VII was not the most popular of monarchs. Having succeeded Richard III, he was forever plagued by threats of rebellion, and if insurgents were to rally to anyone it would be to Edward Plantagenet, the 15-year-old Earl of Warwick and heir to the House of York. The earl was therefore imprisoned in the Tower of London.

Or so it was believed, until one day in November 1486 a young priest from Oxford arrived in Dublin. With him was a handsome youth – none other, said the priest, than the Earl of Warwick, who had managed to escape his London jailers. The boy himself confirmed the story, and disaffected members of the Anglo-Irish aristocracy were only too ready to believe it. Their lord-lieutenant assured them that the young prince who had come among them was England's rightful ruler.

On hearing of this, Henry gave the lie to the story by parading the real earl through the streets of London. This convinced many, but in Ireland it was claimed that the boy produced by Henry was an imposter. And the Irish were not alone. The Earl of Lincoln, nephew of Richard III, was among English noblemen who accepted the story told by the priest and his companion.

Lincoln went to Holland to see his aunt, the Dowager Duchess of Burgundy, sister of Richard III, who detested Henry and wished to see the English throne returned to her own House of York. She also received emissaries from Ireland, and what she heard convinced her that a rebellion favouring the supposed fugitive Earl of Warwick would find support in England. So she raised an army of 2,000 German mercenaries led by Martin Schwartz and despatched them to Ireland. Lincoln, Lord Lovell and other English exiles accompanied them, and shortly after their arrival the priest's protégé was crowned king by the Bishop of Meath at a ceremony in the cathedral church of Dublin.

Edward VI, as he was now styled, arrived with his army on Piel Island, near what is now Barrow, on 4th June 1487. He was accompanied by Lincoln, Lovell and the Earl of Kildare, Ireland's lord-lieutenant, who had added about 5,000 Irish troops to the German mercenaries.

If you wonder how such a tiny island could accommodate so many, the answer is that they didn't stay long. On the same day they continued their journey to the mainland, arriving that night at Swarthmoor, where they were joined by Sir Thomas Broughton, of Broughton-in-Furness, and his retainers.

The next day they marched south, passing through Cartmel and expecting to be joined by growing numbers disenchanted with Henry. But the support they received as they headed first for York fell far short of what was anticipated, and on 16th June they were outnumbered and defeated by Henry's forces. Some 4,000 of the invaders perished, Lincoln and Schwartz among them.

The youth who had been crowned king in Ireland turned out to be Lambert Simnel, the son of a baker. Recognising that he was no more than a pawn in a plot hatched by somebody much higher on the social ladder, Henry decided to make an example rather than a martyr of him and employed him as a kitchen-boy. The young pretender subsequently became one of the king's falconers.

Sir Thomas Broughton was less fortunate. Henry confiscated his estates and gave them to the Earl of Derby, and the dispossessed landowner spent the rest of his life hiding in a cave in woods at Witherslack, where he was supplied with food by faithful servants who on his death buried him nearby.

Trouble
in
Woolpack Yard

JAMES GILPIN was 63, widowed, and needed a housekeeper to look after him and his sons. Elizabeth Nicholson would do nicely, he decided, so she left her home to join the Gilpins at their Kentmere farm.

It was 1884, Elizabeth was 21, and she soon found that her duties were not confined to housekeeping. Gilpin made her his mistress and she bore him five children, although he wouldn't marry her and gave her no wages.

Calling herself 'Mrs Nicholson', she was 39 when Gilpin at last decided to retire at 81 and move to Kendal, where the couple and their children took a cottage in Woolpack Yard, at the rear of the Woolpack Hotel.

Their life was uneventful until a former soldier, Thomas Metcalfe, returned home to live with his stepmother at her cottage in Woolpack Yard. He was 28, and although Mrs Nicholson was now 41 the two soon became lovers. At her suggestion he moved into

her home – unknown to Gilpin, who was now bedridden.

Metcalfe, however, was not a paying guest. He was unemployed, and to keep him Mrs Nicholson was soon dipping into her housekeeping, pawning Gilpin's clothes and then drawing on his bank account. This worried Gilpin's accountant, Alderman John Monkhouse, who was the mayor of Kendal. Mrs Nicholson was exceeding her agreed weekly £3 housekeeping allowance, forging Gilpin's name on cheques. Monkhouse had also heard rumours of her relationship with Metcalfe.

The accountant went to see the couple. He first confronted Mrs Nicholson, who admitted her forgeries when he threatened to report her to the police. Monkhouse then told the old man of the situation. Was he aware, the accountant asked, that a hulking great idle fellow was living under his roof, far better fed and looked after than Gilpin himself?

'It's Tom Metcalfe, who comes to read to you,' Mrs Nicholson told her employer, at the same time assuring Monkhouse, 'It is all lies what people have told you. There is nothing in it.'

The accountant departed after warning her to watch her step, but it wasn't long before she was troubling him again. She needed more money. Monkhouse could guess the reason – she now had not only her lodger's keep to find, but she also had to pay for his increasingly heavy drinking.

The accountant promptly went to see Gilpin, telling him that at the rate Mrs Nicholson was spending his money it would soon all be gone. Metcalfe was still under his roof, and the scandal was becoming the talk of the town.

Although no stranger to scandal himself, Gilpin agreed that something had to be done. Mrs Nicholson must keep Monkhouse informed of all her expenditure, and Metcalfe must leave the house. But attending to this wasn't easy, the old man lamented, as he was unable to get downstairs to keep an eye on what was going on.

Eight days passed, and then Mrs Nicholson called on Monkhouse again. James Gilpin had died, she announced. He had been taken ill with diarrhoea and vomiting. And she thought he had left her £100.

In his role as Gilpin's executor, Monkhouse said that this money had been left not to her, but to the children.

Two days later he received an anonymous letter. It claimed that Mrs Nicholson had purchased blue arsenic at a chemist's opposite Woolpack Yard, and had poisoned James Gilpin. Monkhouse went to the shop, where the chemist confirmed that he had sold blue arsenic to Elizabeth Nicholson, who had said she needed it to kill rats.

Meanwhile, neighbours recalled that for some time Thomas Metcalfe had been saying he was going to marry Elizabeth Nicholson at Easter, and that she would be coming into money when Gilpin died.

Shortly after his return from the chemist's, Monkhouse was visited by Mrs Nicholson. She didn't deny buying the arsenic, but said she had got it to deal with rats, on Gilpin's instructions. The accountant decided to inform the police.

Mrs Nicholson next called on James Gilpin's doctor to pick up the death certificate. The physician was about to complete it when she told him that Richard Gilpin had been saying she had poisoned his father. The doctor put the certificate to one side, telling her she could be in serious trouble if evidence of poisoning were found.

The housekeeper was still out when the police arrived at her home, where Metcalfe was arrested. All he could tell them, he said, was that he had gone to bed with Elizabeth Nicholson in the attic at 10.30 on the night of Gilpin's death. Five hours later Elizabeth had woken him to say she had been down to look at Gilpin, who had been ill, and he was dead.

An autopsy found arsenic in Gilpin's body, and Elizabeth Nicholson still hadn't come home. Police widened their hunt, found her hiding at Metcalfe's brother's cottage in Holme, and took her and Metcalfe to Lancaster prison.

Metcalfe was later discharged. Elizabeth Nicholson was tried at Appleby Assizes in June 1904.

Her defence was simple. She said that Gilpin had told her to get some fat, mix it with the arsenic, spread it on some bread and cheese and put it in the rat holes, just as they had done on the Kentmere farm.

While she was attending to the holes upstairs a neighbour had called and she had gone down to see her, putting the cheese on a chair by the bed. When she returned upstairs and was collecting the cheese, Gilpin told her he had picked up a piece and eaten it. She told him she hoped it wasn't a poisoned piece, and he said that if it was he hadn't eaten enough to harm him.

The county analyst told the court that he had found arsenic in rat holes in the house, but Gilpin had consumed too much of the poison to have taken it by accident.

The court heard that although Elizabeth Nicholson had called the doctor when Gilpin became ill, she had said nothing about the poisoned cheese. One of her daughters said that she had heard Gilpin tell her mother to get the poison, and the defence counsel pointed out that the housekeeper had bought the arsenic openly and had made no attempt to conceal Gilpin's vomit from the doctor. Metcalfe had been in the house, had earlier been heard to say he wished Gilpin were dead, and would have known that Mrs Nicholson had bought the arsenic....

Summing up, the judge told the jury that although Mrs Nicholson had believed she would inherit £100 on Gilpin's death, she must also have realised that at the same time she would lose her housekeeping allowance. And her attempt to hide from the police was not necessarily an indication of guilt – she could have been frightened when the doctor warned her of dire consequences if poison were found.

So was she guilty? The jury decided there was insufficient evidence for them to convict her. Crowds gathered at Kendal station and outside her home that night to await her return, but she was not on the train as expected.

Had she arrived, she might have been surprised by the welcome awaiting her. Local feeling, it was reported, was that Elizabeth Nicholson's acquittal was justified as Metcalfe had not been tried; and, guilty or not, she had been as much sinned against as sinning.

Lovelorn in Coniston

IT was perhaps predictable that the life of the most celebrated of Edwardian romantic novelists would be burnished by fantasy. Of doubtful parentage and a prosaic London background, she changed her name to Marie Corelli, invented an Italian father and a Venetian princess for a mother and went on to make a fortune from her bestsellers. Her conviction that she was the greatest writer of her time led her to make her home in Stratford-upon-Avon, where what had been good enough for Shakespeare fell short of her expectations. Never one to allow drab reality to disappoint her for long, however, she soon suffused Stratford with colour, bowling through the streets at the reins of a victoria drawn by two Shetland ponies and gliding along the river in a gondola imported from Venice, complete with gondolier. As someone observed, she could always be relied upon to act in impeccable bad taste.

She had the money to satisfy most of her whims, but some dreams would forever elude her. It was so when she came to Coniston.

Touring the Lakes in 1906, she sent a message to Brantwood from Coniston's Waterhead Hotel asking if she might visit John Ruskin's former home. Brantwood was now the residence of Arthur Severn, an artist who had married Ruskin's cousin.

The message was delivered, was favourably acknowledged, and the stage was set for one of the more poignant chapters in the novelist's life. She was 51 but contrived to look younger; a trifle plump perhaps, but by no means unprepossessing. Severn was 64 but still cut quite a dashing figure, every inch the artist if not a particularly successful one; and although he could seem aloof and forbidding, he was charm itself with the ladies.

As she stepped from the boat which had brought her across the lake to Brantwood's harbour, Arthur Severn found Marie Corelli to be an intriguing surprise. The feeling was mutual. After a tour of the house and grounds, the novelist and her companion, Bertha Vyver, were invited to return for dinner. Already, Marie's imagination was at work on a classic meeting of kindred spirits, she the gifted author, he the talented painter doomed to obscurity by his dedication to preserving a great man's home. 'Arthur' was no name for such a noble figure. She would call him Pendennis.

And so she did, although this was soon abbreviated to the pet name 'Pen'. The dinner went well, Marie responding to even the trivial with effusive enthusiasm. Before long her hosts were to realise that this was her theatrical reaction to everything. Nevertheless, the friendship burgeoned, Severn flattered by the attention of a celebrity apparently so young – throughout her life, Marie dressed as a girl.

In her diary the novelist recorded the progress of the relationship in terms which might have surprised her hero: theirs was a historic union of souls on a plane altogether higher than the physical ... which perhaps suited Marie Corelli subconsciously, for she was to die a virgin.

LOVELORN IN CONISTON

Severn paid several visits to her Stratford home and she became an occasional guest at Brantwood, staying for a week in 1909, a fortnight in the following year and also at other times. Severn's wife Joan seems to have regarded the situation with an amused but sometimes exasperated tolerance, which found relief in her mimicry of the guest's London diction – 'Ow, Pen, listen to the owells!'

And for Arthur Severn the association began to pall. He became irritated by Marie's affectations and also, perhaps, began to realise that he had been taken up by someone who, despite her wealth and celebrity was something of a joke in the eyes of the discerning. At Sunday worship in Coniston, churchgoers enjoyed the spectacle of companion Bertha in black in attendance on her petite, golden-haired mistress – the pair were compared to a raven and a budgerigar – but at Brantwood Marie Corelli had become what would nowadays be called a pain.

During her last recorded visit Severn retired pointedly to his studio, leaving his wife to entertain the besotted guest. Perhaps it was this slight which ended the 'romance'. For his part, Severn confided to a friend that he could no longer stand the visitor's Cockney accent.

He may also have congratulated himself that with Marie Corelli he had resisted the advice one of her characters gave another: 'Thou wilt not taste life until thou hast sipped the nectar from a pair of rose-red lips.' He was to outlive her by seven years, dying at 89 in 1931. She died at 69, but admitted only to 60.

The
Friends' Friend

THIS is the story of an angel, a messiah and a saint who stopped going to church. Who was who speaks for itself.

The head of the household with which we are concerned was Lord of the Manor of Ulverston, Vice Chancellor of the Duchy of Lancaster and Judge of the Assize for the Chester and North Circuit. So what did this establishment figure do when he came home to find his beautiful wife – little more than half his age – in thrall to a young hot-head bent on reforming the world?

Most husbands and public figures, seeing their marriage and dignity under threat, would have ejected the young upstart, perhaps also using their influence to his disadvantage.

Not so Judge Fell. Instead of stamping firmly on the relationship, he made the newcomer welcome, gave him shelter and used his position to protect him from persecution. The outcome was the founding of a new religious sect – the Quakers, otherwise known as the Society of Friends.

Step into Swarthmoor Hall, the home of Judge Fell in the mid-17th century, and you tread the stage on which this remarkable drama was set. Here it was that George Fox arrived one day in 1652, fresh from his vision of a great throng assembled by the Lord on Pendle Hill. The local independent minister was paying a call and a distinct coolness quickly developed between the two. But Fox made a deep impression upon Margaret Fell, mistress of the house.

A few days later he turned up at Ulverston parish church, was given permission to address the congregation and did so to such effect that he moved Margaret Fell to tears, and a magistrate to have him thrown out.

Meanwhile, Judge Fell was returning from the Welsh circuit, unaware of Fox's arrival and impact on the district. As he completed the perilous crossing of Morecambe Bay sands, the judge was surprised to see a posse of local VIPs, the rector among them, riding out from Kents Bank to meet him. They could hardly wait to tell him their news: his household had been bewitched by an itinerant preacher. Fox must be banished from the area, they urged, before he did any more harm.

Judge Fell, however, had a mind of his own – a mind which, by the standard of his time, was unusually open and was about to be severely tested.

After his long, hazardous and tiring journey he had been looking forward to his customary joyful homecoming. Instead he had been alarmed by Ulverston's harbingers of trouble, and on reaching his fireside he found his family on edge in an atmosphere of uneasiness. Fox's introduction could hardly have been less auspicious. Who could have blamed the judge had he given short shrift to the preacher who had caused such turmoil?

Fox was temporarily absent, but Fell was favourably

impressed by two of the preacher's followers who were also staying at the Hall. Then Fox himself arrived. The judge heard him out and quietly retired for the night. Judgement, it seemed, was suspended. But Margaret sensed the battle had been won, and when the minister called the next day to implore Fell to send Fox packing, he was wasting his time. Had anything further been needed to make up the judge's mind in Fox's favour, this was it. The vociferous minister departed, undone by his own pleading.

Where, the judge heard members of his household asking each other, could they hold meetings for worship? 'You may meet here if you will,' he told them. So they did.

Although he was at one with the Friends in spirit, he never joined them. After a while he ceased attending church, but by not becoming a Quaker he preserved the independence which helped him to shield the Friends from persecution. Religious intolerance, rife at that time, cost many Quakers their lives elsewhere.

As soon as the judge's duties called him away, however, the local establishment took the opportunity to have Fox and his followers harassed and beaten, a process supervised by an Ulverston magistrate and executed by four constables with whips, urged on by a mob.

Nevertheless, by allowing the Friends to use his home and enjoy his protection Judge Fell had been instrumental in nurturing their movement when help was most needed. By the time of his death in 1658, Quakerism was too strong to be eradicated, although its opponents did their best. They searched Swarthmoor Hall, confiscating correspondence and arresting and imprisoning the district's Friends. When Margaret Fell was away from home – either in prison or trying to secure Fox's release – her daughters held the Swarthmoor fort, an island of enlightenment lashed by the waves of a sea of prejudice.

Refusing to stop holding meetings at Swarthmoor Hall, Margaret endured four years' imprisonment in Lancaster Castle until her release was ordered by the king. In 1669, aged 55 and 11 years a widow, she married Fox, who was ten years her junior. But they did not live happily ever after at Swarthmoor Hall for there was work to be done. They continued to advance their cause, she at Swarthmoor and in prison again in Lancaster, he overseas and in London.

George Fox died in 1691, his health broken by his Lancaster incarceration. Margaret followed him 11 years later, home again at Swarthmoor, aged 88 and murmuring, 'I am in peace...'

Today you can walk the garden where Judge Fell paced up and down with the aggrieved minister; step into the parlour where he would sit with the door open so that he could remain apart from and yet be part of the meeting whose sounds reached him from the hall nearby; and you can see some of the yews he planted, one by one, to commemorate the births of his eight daughters – but none remains for the son who grew up to join his mother's persecutors.

The
Croglin Vampire

IT was in 1874 that the Australian brothers Michael and Edward Cranswell and their sister Amelia rented Croglin Grange, in the Vale of Eden. Captain Fisher, their landlord, found them to be good tenants, and they became popular in the village. All went well until one summer night when Amelia went to bed without closing her shutters.

She slept soundly until something, she couldn't say what, awoke her. Going to her window, she was horrified when her gaze was met by two flaming eyes set in a hideous brown face.

The creature outside seemed to be human, but was swathed in shrouds. As it peered at her through the window, its shrivelled fingers scrabbled at the panes. Amelia had locked her door before retiring. Now she wished she hadn't, for in her panic to get out she fumbled at the lock and dropped the key.

Her screams roused her brothers. They broke open Amelia's door and stumbled into her room, to find her lying senseless on the floor. Her neck was bleeding, punctured by what appeared to be marks made by

101

fangs. The brothers rushed to her now-open window, but there was no sign of her attacker.

Amelia's wounds were superficial and she soon regained consciousness, but the Cranswells felt that a temporary change of scene was needed. A long holiday in Switzerland would calm Amelia's shattered nerves, they decided, and they were right. On their return Amelia continued to occupy the same bedroom, although she now took care always to close the shutters at night and to leave the door unlocked. And the brothers kept a gun handy, just in case....

The incident was all but forgotten when, months later, Amelia was woken by the sound of her shutters being forced. Her cries soon brought her brothers to her aid, and Edward dashed outside, gun in hand. He was just in time to see a wraith-like figure fleeing down the drive. He took a shot at it, and the creature stumbled but continued running.

Edward pursued it across frosty fields in the March moonlight and saw it enter Croglin churchyard, where it vanished among the graves. The brother went back to the Grange, returning after dawn to the churchyard, accompanied by several villagers. They discovered that a family vault had been opened. All the coffins inside except one had been disturbed, revealing their skeletal remains.

Opening the undamaged coffin, the searchers found the preserved form of the presumed vampire inside, with a bullet wound in one of its legs. It appeared to be in a coma, and nobody waited for it to come to life. Edward and his helpers lifted it from the coffin, carried it to a corner of the churchyard, built a fire and burned it.

The event was chronicled in the memoirs of Augustus

THE CROGLIN VAMPIRE

Hare (1834–1903), who named Captain Fisher as his source. Sceptics have remarked that there is no Croglin Grange, and that Hare was noted for his susceptibility to the far-fetched. But there is a Croglin Low Hall ... where a ground-floor window has been walled up.

Two Tales
of a Torrent

A IRA FORCE, near Ullswater, was not always approached by the signposted footpath of today. The route has been sympathetically and sensibly 'civilised', with a car park and National Trust café at its foot. Nineteenth-century visitors had different arrangements. 'A stranger approaching from Ulles Water will take a guide at Lyulph's Tower, and be conducted along the brow of the ravine to the bridges,' said an 1859 tourists' handbook.

And that's how it was when the writer Thomas de Quincey lived at Grasmere, heard the story of one of those Aira Force visitors, and in the 1830s chronicled it for posterity.

Thinking she knew the area well enough, Miss Elizabeth Smith decided to manage without a guide; so she didn't call at Lyulph's Tower, the Duke of Norfolk's hunting lodge, from which one or other of the gamekeeper's family would lead tourists up the footpath to view the 60 foot plunge of Aira Force.

Miss Smith, however, was not a tourist. She lived not far away, and she wanted to do some sketching – not just of Aira Force, but also other scenes in the vicinity – and she didn't want the encumbrance of a companion. By the time she reached her first vantage point, all trace of the footpath had vanished, but she was sure-footed and decided to press on, making her way round and over rocks as she continued her ascent.

Reaching the brink of the chasm, she found there was no further way up ... and when she turned to retrace her steps, she could see no safe way to descend. In a panic, she looked this way and that but could see nothing but vertical rocks. She sat down to recover her composure, rising after a brief rest to scan the skyline in the hope of spotting a shepherd. But the fells were deserted.

Finding no sign of help on the horizon, she looked around her again and was surprised to see a young woman in a white muslin robe, standing about 200 yards away on the other side of the force. The woman beckoned her, indicating a way down the steep incline which Miss Smith had overlooked in her confusion. With new-found confidence, and steadying herself with her collapsible sketching-stool which folded up to form a walking-stick, Miss Smith followed the directions of the woman in white, who indicated where she should approach the edge of the force's chasm, and where the route departed from it.

As the sketcher drew closer to her guide, she saw that the girl was her sister, who now directed her to a platform of rock from which she could see the footpath from which she had strayed. Pausing to recover her breath, she turned to thank her sister, but now there was no sign of her.

Having seen that she was safe, her sister must have gone on ahead, thought Miss Smith. But it was odd that she hadn't waited to keep her company on the long walk home. Sure enough, however, the sister was there when a tired Miss Smith arrived home two hours later. But she knew nothing of Elizabeth's adventure. She had been at home throughout the sketcher's absence, as the rest of the family confirmed. . . .

Lyulph's Tower, which Miss Smith neglected to visit, had been built by the tenth Duke of Norfolk in 1780. It stands on a site believed to have been formerly occupied by a pele-tower, a building associated with a legend celebrated by Wordsworth in his poem *The Somnambulist*.

The original tower was supposedly the home of Lady Emma Howard, one of the Howards of Greystoke. Her beauty attracted numerous suitors, from whom she chose one Sir Eglamore, exchanging vows of undying love beneath a holly tree above Aira Force. Their marriage was postponed, however, because Eglamore felt that he should first make a name for himself with feats of knight-errantry. He accordingly went abroad in search of adventure, while Lady Emma languished at home, hearing occasional reports of his exploits overseas, and then nothing for months on end.

Tortured by anxiety and suspicious of her knight's fidelity, she began sleep-walking, making always for the spot where the two had declared their love. But Eglamore had not been unfaithful. At last he returned, unannounced and late at night – so late, that rather than rouse the household at Lyulph's Tower, he went to the holly tree near the force and lay down to sleep.

Before long, footsteps woke him and he saw Lady Emma standing nearby in her white nightgown, plucking leaves from the holly tree and casting them into the force. Eglamore arose, walked quietly to her side, put out a hand and gently touched her. Startled into consciousness, she let out a scream, took a false step and toppled headlong into the torrent.

Plunging after her, Eglamore dragged her from the water. She opened her eyes. She recognized him. She knew he had been faithful after all, but it was too late. Within minutes, she was dead.

In his grief, Sir Eglamore built a hut near the force, and lived out the rest of his days there, as a recluse.

Last Orders
in Seathwaite

THE secluded hamlet of Seathwaite in the Duddon valley is quite the last place where you might imagine an ugly scene, let alone a riot with a murder trial as its sequel. And in the 20th century, too!

The story begins with water and moves on to something a little stronger. It also has much to do with a former peculiarity of this village – until 1971 its pub was also a post office.

Barrow-in-Furness needed water, and shortly after the turn of the century Seathwaite Tarn in the fells above the village was selected as the site for a reservoir. Navvies arrived, construction commenced and for a while the local economy benefited from the influx of labour.

Like many of their calling, however, the navvies enjoyed a drink and didn't always know when to stop. Sometimes that decision had to be taken for them, as on 25th July 1904.

It had been a hot day, enough to make anyone thirsty. It was also pay-day for the reservoir's builders and this they had begun to celebrate at the Traveller's Rest down the valley in Ulpha. Darkness had fallen by the time they set out to make their vociferous but less than steady way back to Seathwaite. Their approach was evident long before they arrived. Thomas Dawson, landlord of the Newfield Inn, was among those who heard them coming.

As they reeled into Seathwaite they felt in need of topping-up. Dawson felt they'd already had more than enough. He refused to serve them. It was one of those decisions which seem right at the time but are open to question in retrospect. Had the landlord obliged, there might well have been a drunken brawl or two, a few shattered beer glasses and perhaps the odd broken window. But that was nothing compared with what was to happen.

Outraged by Dawson's rejection, the navvies proceeded to vent their anger not just on the pub but also on the village. Picking up whatever lay to hand, some began hurling missiles at the inn's windows, others had a go at the church and vicarage. Police Sergeant Kay and his dog, a team adept at locating drunks in ditches, were not on hand and this was perhaps just as well. Their presence might only have further inflamed the situation.

While the inn's staff sought safety on a hayrick in a nearby barn, the landlord and his daughter took more positive action. Poking shotguns through their shattered windows they blazed away to such effect that one rioter was killed and two were wounded.

Thomas Dawson's trial for murder was the sequel. Guess why he was acquitted. The Newfield Inn, remember, was also a post office. He pleaded that he had been defending Crown property, and this was accepted.

Cartmel's
Bold Defenders

CARLISLE had fallen. News of the Scots' invasion reached Cartmel on 22nd November 1745. Parish dignitaries hastily convened a meeting, deciding that at 9 am the next day all Cartmel's able-bodied men should assemble on the summit of Hampsfield Fell. And so they did, supplementing the few guns to be found in the parish with agricultural implements and kitchen utensils. Veterans of the 1715 invasion were among the throng, doing their best to forget that earlier debacle – on seeing the advancing Highlanders, the Cumberland and Westmorland Militia had turned and fled. This time it would be different, everyone assured each other. They wouldn't like to be in the shoes of any Scots rebel who dared to march on Cartmel.

Harry Barwick, a racehorse owner, was deputed to take the fleetest mount from his stable and dash along the sands from Grange to Milnthorpe. When he sighted the invaders he was to hasten back to give Cartmel due warning. By 10 am he was on his way.

As the hours passed and there was no sign of him, the defenders of Cartmel became increasingly anxious. Had he been captured or his retreat cut off? Tension mounted. Then at 4 pm the observer with the most powerful spy-glass cried: 'I see a horseman galloping quickly round the farthest point ... it's Barwick! He's without his hat and coat! He gallops for life! His horse is covered with foam, as white as snow!'

What happened next was chronicled by the Cartmel historian James Stockdale, whose grandmother had been evacuated to Yorkshire to escape the invasion. 'With livid faces and hair on end,' he recorded, Cartmel's defenders 'rushed to and fro irresolute, not knowing what to do. At length one or two began to leave the crest of the fell...'

All at once the remainder 'in a dense and confused mass violently rushed pell-mell down the precipitous hill, tumbling over each other, heads over heels and heels over heads, in the most ludicrous way. Arms of all kinds, hats, shoes, bonnets and even the loose stones and rocks on the sides of the hill joining in the mêlée...'

Reaching the narrow lane leading to Cartmel, they jammed each other against the walls and hedges in their flight. And on arriving home 'they barricaded themselves in with chairs, tables and everything else that was loose, and creeping into nooks and corners and under the very beds, they bated their breath and waited, as they thought, their doom.'

After all, tradition had handed down to them what happened when Robert the Bruce entered Cartmel in 1322. Only the priory had been spared and tales were told of houses burned and girls carried off to Scotland, half-naked at sword point.

Meanwhile Harry Barwick soon reached Hampsfield Fell and was surprised to find no one awaiting him and signs all around of the townsfolk's flight. Galloping on into Cartmel, he reduced the inhabitants to even greater terror, the clatter of his horse's hooves being taken for the arrival of a mounted Scots regiment.

Finding the streets deserted and all doors shut fast, he walked his horse to the market cross and looked about him in astonishment. Then the silence was broken by an old woman peering from the highest window in the Gateway Tower above him.

'Oh, Harry Borrik, is that ye?' she asked. 'Whaare er t'Scotch?'

Scotch? cried Harry. How the devil should he know? He'd seen none since he left Cartmel.

Then why, asked the woman, had he galloped back so fast?

He thought he'd try the pluck of Cartmel, Harry replied – see what mettle its folk were made of, and now he knew they were 'nowt but dross'.

But Cartmel had not been alone in fearing invasion. The defenders of Whitehaven had pulled down bridges, broken up roads and blockaded entrances to the town, all valuables in shops and houses being transferred to ships lying offshore, to be taken to Dublin or the Isle of Man at the first sight of the Scots. And unknown to the residents of Cartmel, on the day they took fright at the sight of Harry Barwick charging back along the sands, more than 6,000 rebels had marched into Kendal.

A
Man of Iron

HENRY WILLIAM SCHNEIDER was a commuter. His workplace was about 25 miles from his home, and his journeys were made in the 19th century when travel was less sophisticated than it is today. But don't feel sorry for him. It was, after all, by choice that he lived in Bowness when his office was in Barrow. And his commuting was no strap-hanging ordeal. You or I might even have done it for pleasure.

His day began at Belsfield, his 16-bedroom residence which stood in eight acres and was maintained by a staff of more than 40. He had moved here from Ulverston in 1869, after the expansion of the Furness Railway made commuting to Barrow feasible.

On setting out from home he would be preceded by his butler bearing his breakfast on a silver tray. This would be consumed in the saloon of his steam yacht as it carried him down Lake Windermere to Lakeside on the far shore, where his train with his own special coach waited to whisk him to Barrow, a town he had been largely responsible for creating.

He had first come to the Lake District on holiday as a young Londoner in 1839. His Swiss grandfather had settled in England in the previous century, prospering as

a merchant and establishing a business which expanded to include mining interests in Britain, South America, Mexico and Australia. Young Henry William – whose accomplishments included adding up six columns simultaneously – thus came to know a lot about mining. He knew that Furness was rich in haematite ore deposits, although individually these tended to be small. Nobody had made a really big strike.

With prospecting in his blood, H.W. Schneider acquired mining rights in the area, the family firm allocating £50,000 for exploration. Years passed as their Furness prospecting brought inadequate returns. Success eluded them as one promising site after another yielded no more than a paltry tonnage and it seemed that the money would have been better invested elsewhere. It had all but run out when Schneider decided to make one last effort at Park, near Dalton.

The area had been prospected unsuccessfully ten years earlier, but locals assured him that a lot of ore was there if only it could be found. It continued to be elusive and Schneider was about to pull out, his budget spent, when his men offered to work a further week for nothing. A new shaft was sunk and the richest deposit in all Furness was discovered.

It became the foundation of an enterprise which brought prosperity to the area, encouraging Schneider to develop other Furness interests. His firm had already bought several small mines in the district, their output helping to fund further exploration. Now the village of Barrow was to become an iron and steel boom town.

Although Schneider was an autocrat used to having his own way, he was a benevolent despot, his generosity well known. Nobody was more public-spirited. He devoted so much time to serving on committees and fulfilling the duties of various public offices in his work for the community that it was a wonder that he was also able to be a successful businessman. So why didn't he become Sir Henry Schneider, at the least?

The answer lies in his political ambition, which led to his disgrace. He lived in an age when political corruption was commonplace, prospective MPs buying votes at election time; and it was his misfortune that the conduct of the hustings in Lancaster in the general election of 1865 was singled out for examination by a Royal Commission.

Schneider had retained his seat as one of the two MPs for Lancaster, and it transpired that both had bribed the voters, Schneider devoting £1,000 in gold sovereigns to that purpose. The election was consequently declared void and Lancaster was disenfranchised, Schneider having also to resign as a Deputy Lieutenant of Lancashire and a magistrate.

Not that Barrow thought any the less of him. Four years after his death in 1887 the town erected his statue, complete with mayoral robes. No one had done more for the place.

Gough's Dog

WHOEVER heard of a dog being libelled? Cumbria did. The dog was falsely accused of eating its master. It was on 18th April 1805 that its story began when it set off at the heel of its owner, Charles Gough, a young man from Manchester holidaying in the Lake District for some fishing and sketching.

They had taken refreshment at a pub in Patterdale, where Gough had asked for a guide to lead him over the mountains to Wythburn, but none was available – they were all taking part in a review of the Volunteers at Penrith.

Thinking he knew the area well enough, however, Gough set out with his dog to scale Helvellyn. His departure from Patterdale was soon followed by a hailstorm and fog, and no more was heard of him until 20th July, when a shepherd gathering sheep on Helvellyn was startled to hear a dog bark and went to investigate.

By Red Tarn, below the precipice of Cove Head, he found a small, half-starved dog beside a man's skeleton. What had once been the man's clothes had been reduced to a few strips of rag and his skull was missing, but was later found some distance away. The dog, variously described as a spaniel or terrier bitch, had pupped during its three-month vigil. Its dead puppies lay

117

nearby. The human remains were identified as those of Charles Gough from his name inscribed on his gold watch. His hat had been cut in two, indicating that he had probably died instantly, striking his head on falling from the crag. His bones appeared so light, to one man attending the interment, 'that it would not have been difficult to have borne them to the grave under one's arm.'

Both Wordsworth and Sir Walter Scott devoted poems to the tragedy and the dog's fidelity, but some press accounts presented a different view.

The *Carlisle Journal* reported: 'The bitch had pupped in a furze bush near the body of her master and, shocking to relate, had torn the cloaths from the body and eaten him to a perfect skeleton.' Similarly, the *Cumberland Pacquet* noted: 'It appears that a small brown bitch, which accompanied him, had pupped after the fatal event: which, together with her litter, was found near his remains, uncommonly fat! And the flesh of the latter was mostly consumed.'

Both those reports were peppered with inaccuracies, however, and a correspondent of the *Pacquet* subsequently announced: 'In contradiction of the report that the dog had eaten his master, I have to state, from the opinion of some well-informed people in the neighbourhood, that from the frequency of the carcases of animals being devoured by birds of prey (which assemble there in great numbers), there can be little doubt that his body had fallen a sacrifice to those voracious birds.'

Canon H.D. Rawnsley of Keswick, preparing to have a memorial stone placed at the spot, made exhaustive inquiries and could not find one person who thought the dog could have eaten its master. All those he questioned believed that such an act was not in a dog's nature – folk might as well talk, said one veteran Helvellyn shepherd, of a child eating its dead father or mother. It was more likely, the locals believed, that Gough's companion had survived by feeding on sheep carrion on the fells, which would be plentiful at that time of the year. Ravens were more probable culprits. And a Grasmere man who had gone to the scene and subsequently helped the Goughs with the funeral arrangements had nothing but praise for the 'faithful bitch' and confirmed that her pups were found dead.

Nevertheless, the *Globe* reported: 'It is notorious in Patterdale that the men who actually found the remains of poor Gough answered the question that puzzled Wordsworth, as to with what food the animal was sustained during the months that elapsed before its master's body was found, without any difficulty whatever.'

A dog eating its master was more dramatic than one merely guarding the body for three months, so why spoil a good story with the facts? After all, a dog couldn't sue. . . .

Unwelcome Guests

IN the 1990s Dalton-in-Furness acquired a bypass ...
three-and-a-half centuries too late. Had the town
been bypassed in 1631, it might have been spared much
suffering. The vicar might not have lost more than half
his congregation, and Dalton might have endured as a
prosperous market town. But there was no need for a
bypass in 1631. There was no traffic problem and
nowhere of much consequence between Dalton and the
Irish Sea – Furness Abbey had long since been dissolved
and the creation of Barrow awaited the Industrial
Revolution. Had there been a bypass, however, Dalton
might have escaped the attention of two visitors from
London. Seldom could strangers have been less
welcome.

George Postlethwaite, schoolmaster and parish clerk,
recorded the arrival of 'a miserably accursed vile fugitive
named Lancaster with his wife who came down from the
superb city of London, bearing his own shafts of death
enclosed amongst garments which were to destroy many
of the living. They brought in their baggage a tartarean
plague.'

Hitherto, Dalton had been fortunate when there were

national epidemics. There was little through traffic and Dalton's defence against disease was its comparative isolation. But isolated communities tend also to be close communities in which everyone is at least on nodding terms, and it is in such situations that infections flourish.

There were those who regarded the newcomers with suspicion, for London was known to be less than healthy, but the Lancasters had no trouble finding lodgings. Then the plague made itself known, swiftly and virulently, and townsfolk sought to escape by fleeing to the surrounding countryside, moving out to nearby villages or seeking refuge with relatives further away. Dalton's church stood empty, its vicar gone.

George Postlethwaite also left in a hurry, but Lancaster remained. Assisted by an aristocratic friend, he busied himself collecting corpses on a ladder, taking them to communal graves into which they were tipped without ceremony. Whether or not he was inadvertently responsible for the epidemic, he now seemed to be trying to make amends. Certainly, he was setting an example which few townsfolk cared to follow. Gone was the traditional friendliness of the community, superseded by fear and suspicion of anyone who seemed ill. The sick who could once have counted on assistance from neighbours now found themselves avoided.

When the reason for the exodus from Dalton became known outside, armed guards were placed on surrounding roads to halt the evacuation and prevent the plague from spreading. In the stricken town nine died in a single night, 60 in just over a week. By now Lancaster and his wife were blamed by all for bringing the plague. He carried on burying the dead, and was perhaps tolerated for performing the service others were loth to undertake; Mrs Lancaster stayed indoors to avoid both the plague and her neighbours' insults. The couple were to be among the survivors, perhaps inoculated against infection by having previously suffered a milder strain of the virus in London.

But as the epidemic reached the end of its course their troubles were not over. On the orders of a magistrate, Lancaster and his aristocratic assistant were thrown into prison. Then the scandalised community discovered that the pair had been stockpiling sheets and clothing of the deceased in a local granary.

When Lancaster and his wife finally left Dalton they tried to slip away unnoticed. They were not successful. Residents stoned and beat them and Lancaster would probably have been killed had he not held his breath to feign death.

After the couple's departure Dalton carried out a late spring-clean, burning everything suspected of contamination. But much of the town's trade had gone to Ulverston, never to be regained.

The
Terrible
Trencherman

ALL was quiet at the King's Head in Broughton-in-Furness. It was 1 pm, and it seemed that the village was taking a siesta that summer afternoon, for the inn had no customers ... until a man came striding down the road, a knapsack on his back, a sprig of laburnum in the band of his felt hat, and dust on his double-soled boots which told of a long hike.

Entering the inn's lobby, he stepped into the parlour and eased off his knapsack. Then, ringing the bell for attention, he took a seat by the window, overlooking the sunlit street.

The parlour door opened to admit Sally, the serving-girl. He'd like a pint of best ale, said the walker. and what could she offer him to eat? Sally said she'd go and see. When she returned, the man had lit his pipe at the open window.

'Please, sir,' she said, 't' missus says there's a goose at t' fire, and ye can dine off that if ye can wait a bit.'

'A goose! What a feast! Good – tell your mistress that I'll wait.'

123

THE TERRIBLE TRENCHERMAN

The bird duly arrived, served by the landlady herself. Left alone with it, the walker carved himself a portion and ate his fill. The greater part of the goose remained but, hungry though he had been, the man could manage no more.

From his seat at the window, he saw the first sign of life in the quiet street. A gipsy tinker approached and passed, followed by another. Then the gipsies' cart appeared, drawn by an unkempt pony led by a boy. Under the cart's tarpaulin the walker could see a huddle of children and an elderly woman. Beside the cart walked a tall, middle-aged woman, a red handkerchief tied over her raven-black hair. Seeing the man at the window, she left the side of the cart and approached.

'God bless your honour's bonny face!' she said. 'There's good fortune before ye!'

'God bless *you*,' said the walker, leaning out to drop a shilling in her palm. 'Are those your children in the cart?'

'Four of them, your honour.'

'Wait a minute,' said the walker, glancing quickly up and down the road. There was nobody else about, and the cart had come to a rest. Grabbing the plate with the remains of the goose, he carried it to the window. 'Now, hold out your apron!' he told the woman.

From the cart, she produced a tartan shawl, holding one corner in her teeth, and two more in her outstretched hands. In a trice, the walker swept the goose from the dish and into the shawl below him.

'Now be off,' he said, 'as fast as you can.'

Bundling the goose into the cart, the woman whispered to the boy with the horse, 'Drive on – quick!'

Closing the window, the man returned to his table, lit

his pipe and rang the bell.

'You may clear away the things,' he told Sally. 'I've finished.'

'Yes, sir,' said the girl. Then her eyes fell on the empty dish. For a moment, she stood transfixed. She picked up the dish, and put it down again. A fork dropped to the floor, and as she bent to retrieve it she looked for the bird's carcase under the table. Nothing was there, nor in the fireplace.

Rising from the floor, she gazed wide-eyed at the diner. 'Did ye say ye'd finished, sir?' she asked in confusion.

'Yes. You may clear the table. And let me know what I have to pay.'

'What ye hev to pay? Yes, sir,' said Sally, giving him a scared look as she hurried out to the kitchen, where the landlord now sat alone.

'It's all gone!' she cried.

'What's all gone?'

'The goose! He's etten the lot – bones an' all!'

The landlord gave a low whistle. 'Well!' he said, taking a puff at his pipe. 'All I hev to say is, if I'm wick an' hearty when that man dees, I'll be glad to go to his berrin', in mi best clo'es, whether I'm axed or not. Didsta say t' bones an' all?'

'Bones an' all!' repeated the girl.

'Arta right in thi yed, thinksta?'

'It's true, I tell ye! An' he says I'm to clear t' table!'

'Doesta hear what shoo says?' asked the landlord as his wife entered the kitchen.

'What is it?'

'He's etten all t' goose!'

'Who hes?'

'Yon divulskin in t' parlour!'

'I nivver heard the like!'

'Nor me nawther.'

'It's quite ta'en mi breath.'

'Mine, too. An' he wants to knaw what he hes to pay. What thinksta?'

'Think? I knaw not what to think. It caps me completely.'

'Didsta notice ony difference about t' fit of his waistcoat?' the landlord asked Sally.

'Nay.'

'Well then, he must hev a terrible cavity somewhere in his inside. Didsta say he was a gentleman?'

'He *looks* like a gentleman.'

'Well, that's a blessin' – for no poor body could maintain sich a wolf as he keeps in his coat. A man like that should hev somebody runnin' a day's march afore him, to scrape his proven together. We cannot charge him less nor t' price o' t' goose.'

'He shouldna grummle at that,' said the landlady.

'I should think not – he's t' reason of a man, surely, if he's t' stomach of a horse.'

'I nivver heard tell of a horse eatin' goose.'

'Nivver mind that. Sally, gan thi ways an' tell him it'll be seven shillin'.'

Declaring his meal cheap at the price, the stranger insisted on paying ten shillings, adding a shilling tip for the girl, and asking the landlord to join him for a glass of wine, to give him directions to Little Langdale by way of the Duddon valley.

As the two sat talking by the open window, curious townsfolk gathered below. Thanks to Sally, news of the stranger who had consumed a whole goose, bones included, was already the talk of all Broughton.

Whispered conversations outside the pub could be heard from the window.

'I'd give an odd shillin' to see him feed. ...'

'I wonder where he's bin browt up.'

'Somewhere where there's nae stint. He's nae mountain grazer, that yan.'

'I tell ye what, lads – he'd be a terrible piece o' furniture in a poor man's house.'

Long after the stranger's departure, his feat was recalled with awe. And when he returned three years later, saying he'd lost his appetite and telling the landlord the truth of the matter, Broughton preferred the original version.

When did this happen? Sometime before 1874 when the story was told by Edwin Waugh, who identified the landlord as Adam Ritson, a native of Seathwaite and in his day a prizewinning Cumbrian wrestler.